Manage Revenue

By Johan Hammer

Johan@revenuesuperstar.com
Instagram: revenuesuperstar

ISBN: 9781791727642

© **Copyright 2018 - All rights reserved.**

The contents of this book may not be reproduced, duplicated, or transmitted without direct written permission from the author.

Under no circumstances will any legal responsibility or blame be held against the publisher for any reparation, damages, or monetary loss due to the information herein, either directly or indirectly.

Legal Notice:
You cannot amend, distribute, sell, use, quote, or paraphrase any part of the content within this book without the consent of the author.

Disclaimer Notice:
By reading this document, the reader agrees that under no circumstances is the author responsible for any losses, direct or indirect, which are incurred as a result of the use of information contained within this document, including, but not limited to, errors, omissions, or inaccuracies.

Table of Contents

Introduction 3

What is Revenue Management? 7

ONE - Data 13

TWO - Learn the Basics 25

THREE - Pricing and Optimization 43

FOUR - Value 53

FIVE - Rocket Science and Wishful Thinking 61

SIX - Booking Windows 71

SEVEN - Group Pricing and Displacement 79

EIGHT - More Optimization 85

PART 2 - Bonus Chapters 95

Rate Leakage 97

What is AI? 103

How Can I Increase My Average Rates? 109

Tricks to Increase Profit Margin 115

Tips on Improving Computer Skills 117

Recommended Reads for Revenue Managers 121

Glossary of Terms 125

Works Cited 139

About the Author

Johan Hammer has more than ten years of experience in the hospitality industry, including over seven years of revenue management experience.

Most recently, in June 2017, Johan co-founded a travel startup called Instaroom where they help hotels with conversational bookings through messaging, which enables the hotels to unlock new revenue opportunities and enhanced guest experiences on their website. Thousands of travelers rely on Instaroom to make their bookings.

Messaging is here to stay. After all, research shows that at least 88% of people born after 1981 prefer communicating via messaging.

Feel free to reach out to Johan at johan@instaroom.travel to learn more and to get a free trial of Instaroom (www.instaroom.travel) for your hotel or brand.

His previous endeavor was as a Revenue & Distribution Specialist for a large Scandinavian hotel chain, First Hotels. Johan's main role there was to consult with hotels regarding revenue and distribution-related matters. He also internally analyzed and suggested new strategies for the brand and its stakeholders.

In 2015, Johan earned a certificate from Cornell University after completing their course titled, *Advanced Hospitality Revenue Management: Pricing and Demand Strategies*.

Introduction

"If they won't write the kind of books we like to read, we shall have to write them ourselves."
C. S. Lewis
Author of *The Chronicles of Narnia*

The purpose of this book is to provide a basic understanding of the essential principles behind successful revenue management and how to effectively apply these principles in your hotel. The definition of a revenue manager can vary a lot from hotel to hotel. The purpose of this book is not to define the job description of a revenue manager but to define the basic principles of revenue management that have proven to stand the test of time. These are principles that I have successfully used in my own career as a hotel revenue manager. The revenue management and distribution scenes evolve at a rapid pace; my goal is to make sure this guide will be as relevant in 10 years as it is in 2018. I will do my utmost to ensure this goal is achieved.

I compiled a list of eight essential skills that I believe all revenue managers should practice. If you feel something is missing from this list, you are probably correct. This list is based on my own experience, academic studies, and observations of how the very best revenue managers do it.

This book is written for beginners as well as experienced hospitality professionals. See it as your playbook to use and revert back to whenever you need guidance.

In my previous book, *Revenue Superstar!* I answered some of the most frequently asked questions I got as a revenue manager. Instead of making another book that simply answers questions, I've designed this book to give you the step-by-step framework to practice successful revenue management. If you already read *Revenue Superstar!* there will be some repetition in this book; feel free to skip ahead if you already understand these concepts.

When I first started my career as a revenue manager, I was looking for a book like this—something that was easy to follow along with and was hands-on and cutting to the core of the RM practice without confusing the reader with complicated acronyms. I was not successful in my quest of finding such a book and that is why you are reading this book today.

As far as my working practice is concerned, I have a strange desire to put myself into complicated situations in order to figure out the best solutions. Once I find a solution, I like to simplify it and package it so others can easily understand it.

As Einstein so elegantly put it, *"Everything should be made as simple as possible, but not simpler."*

What is Revenue Management?

"Without data, you're just another person with an opinion."
W. Edwards Deming

Revenue management is all about maintaining and optimizing the hotel's revenue streams to ensure revenue growth. This is achieved by making data-driven decisions. One example of this is by forecasting future demand and making necessary adjustments and actions to reach the hotel's target.

Our main product (hotel rooms) is often referred to as a perishable inventory. In other words, you hold an inventory of perishable products. The definition of perishable inventory in the case of hotel rooms basically means that if we do not sell the rooms we have available for tonight, they will disappear. We cannot sell those rooms tomorrow. Later in the book we will discuss booking windows and time value which will be an essential skill to manage this kind of complex inventory.

At the end of the day, it is about selling the room to the one who needs it the most; however, that doesn't mean that the potential buyer who "needs it the most" actually knows that you exist. The role as a revenue manager is to anticipate future hotel performance and the market, and by using a data-and-action-driven mindset, create momentum to ensure your hotel is in front of the right buyer at the right time. This involves a variety of skills such as action-based forecasting, understanding booking windows, daily pricing optimization while ensuring the most cost-efficient channels, and more. But don't worry, as promised, I will go over all the steps in this book. Once you finish the book, it's up to you to set them in motion in your own hotel.

There is a human psychological tendency called the *availability bias*, which refers to the bias a person's mind has toward recent examples when making a difficult decision. What happens is that we often substitute a difficult question with an easier one. For example, you may ask the question: "Will we reach our budget target next month?" That's a difficult question. Then you might ask yourself: "Did we reach our target for the same period last year?" If the answer is yes to the second question, the answer to the first question also becomes yes.

So, in other words, when we are faced with a hard question, we tend to be tricked into relying on what we already know about this easier question instead of finding the right/correct facts. A better question would be: do I have enough information to know if we will reach our target for next month?

Your role as a revenue manager is to be a hungry, data-driven general who combines your own experience with data. Once you have some experience to lean back on, this is an unbeatable formula for success.

To learn more about these psychological tendencies, I recommend reading "Thinking Fast and Slow" by Daniel Kahneman and Misbehaving: The Making of Behavioral Economics by Richard Thaler. Both authors have won the Nobel Prize for their studies in the field of behavioural economics. This field is very much connected with our industry.

80/20 Rule of Revenue Management

"Power law distributions are so big that they hide in plain sight."
Peter Thiel -
PayPal co-founder

The first step toward proper revenue management is to understand that some tasks are more valuable than others. Every single principle in this book qualifies for the 80/20 rule. This is a very simple rule and you have probably heard of it before, but as seen in the quote above, it can very easily hide in plain sight. I believe it's worth revisiting before we jump to the next part of the book.

The Pareto Principle
The Pareto Principle derives its name from Vilfredo Pareto, the economist who first discerned the principle's existence. The principle explains how an unequal relationship exists between inputs and outputs, wherein for many phenomena, 20% of invested inputs are responsible for 80% of the results obtained. This is known as the *80/20 rule*.

Get the basics right and the principles in this book will be the 20% that stands for 80% of your success.

A simple example of the 80/20 rule: Which 20% of your hotel's distribution channels stands for 80% of the reservations? This is where to focus time and money when setting up campaigns or promotions. Do not focus on the trivial many; instead, focus on the vital few. Focus on what hides in plain sight.

PARETO PRINCIPLE

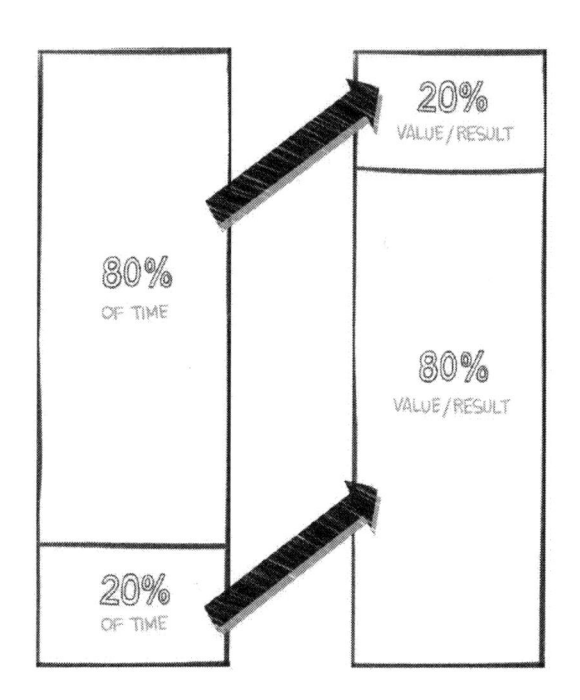

80% OF TIME → 20% VALUE/RESULT

20% OF TIME → 80% VALUE/RESULT

ONE

Data

I dare to claim that *revenue manager* is just the industry name for *hotel data scientist*. You are the expert who should be able to take raw data and turn it into actionable insight. You are the one who must find the signal within the noise. Obviously there is a lot of great analytics software out there but you must know the basics. Otherwise, you wouldn't know where to focus your attention.

Everything you do on a daily basis is related to data and being able to decipher and understand what the data can tell you. The quality of the data is, therefore, extremely important. Shit in, shit out. This was something I learned quickly. If the quality of the data is poor, you will make decisions based on false information.

What data am I talking about? I will not go into details just yet but here's a simple example.

If new reservations get incorrectly segmented, it might affect your statistics in a way that your future decisions are based on false predictions. If this happens once, no problem, but if there's a consistent glitch, it will turn into false trends and someone might take action on these false insights.

You are a data-driven general. Gut feeling is only good if you have enough experience and you combine it with data.

Hence, it is very important to set up automatic and manual procedures on a daily, weekly, and monthly basis to make sure new reservations have the correct rate codes, rate categories, segments, etc.

Did you know that in 2013, 90% of the world's data was created in the previous two years? According to ScienceDaily, 80% of that is what is called unstructured data (clicks, comments, posts, likes etc.). The amount of data we get access to only increases and it can be daunting to know which data points and KPIs are actually important to look at.

Which Numbers Are Important?

Before we move to the next chapter to discuss getting the basics right, I will share a chapter from my previous book *Revenue Playbook!* where I discuss which KPIs are important and how to judge certain data points with a simple technique called the Triple-A rule. Don't worry if you think we are moving into details too fast. Some of these concepts will be explained in more detail later in the book. I thought it would be a nice example to include while we are on the topic of data. In the following exercise, we look at how to be able to focus on signal over noise.

Revenue Management

Not all KPIs—and numbers (the data) in general—are equally important. This probably does not come as a surprise to you, but you may still wonder what numbers are actually important enough to measure on a daily and weekly basis. The numbers that you will want to focus on are the ones that give you enough actionable insights to help you optimize your hotel's revenue streams.

To determine which numbers you should utilize most regularly, apply the Triple-A rule. Think of the numbers that meet the requirements of the Triple-A rule this way:
- They must be **Actionable**
  The data should provide clear direction for strategic and managerial decisions.
- They must be **Accessible**
- The data should be simple to find and simple to read.
- They must be **Auditable**
- The data must be real in the sense that it is derived from clean and accurate data sources.

Obviously, the numbers you choose will be closely connected to your overarching revenue-management strategy.

My highly biased recommendation, however, is to monitor the following RM KPIs very closely, as each has a strong correlation with higher hotel profitability. Furthermore, each of these KPIs is

universal, and thus probably hold true for most hotels. They include:
- Hotel satisfaction score
- Pickup (often confused with pace)
- Booking pace
- ADR (Average Daily Rate)

You might think that it's strange to not see RGI (RevPAR) index on my list. RevPAR index is what we use when we compare the hotel's revenue performance to a set of competitors or the market as a whole. It gives you an idea of whether your hotel is getting its fair share of what the market is offering. In a perfect world, all hotels would have a RevPAR index of 1.0.

But let's see if RevPAR meets the Triple-A rule's criteria.

Is the RevPAR Index Actionable? Well, not really. It gives you an idea of whether your hotel is performing well and if your occupancy and average rate are good or bad compared with your competitors. But the index, or RevPAR itself, doesn't tell you what your competitors are doing differently or what you need to do to win market shares; it's not detailed enough. It's very difficult to see from this number alone if your competitors perform better because they have more corporate accounts than you do or if it's because they pay for preferred placement on sites like Booking.com. Do they have a mix of business with more "expensive" bookings? Expensive refers to distribution costs such as commissions, delivery costs, and so forth. In that sense, the RevPAR index itself doesn't give you enough *actionable* insights.

Is it Accessible? This one is an emphatic Yes! It's very easy to find, and once you are instructed on how to read it, it's easy to remember.

Is it Auditable? Well, yes and no. Sometimes hotels use a manual process for entering data, and sometimes, as a result, they might forget to deduct or include things like breakfast costs. This might provide you with false indications as to how your competitors are performing. Also, as mentioned above, it's difficult to know what kind of business your competitors have. Therefore, it's hard to know if you actually are doing better than they are, even if your index score is objectively lower. A lower index score may actually be the result of having a more profitable business mix with lower costs.

As you can see, the RevPAR index doesn't entirely live up to the Triple-A rule.

Now, let's have a look at the revenue management KPIs that I recommend and let's see if they pass the Triple-A test.

Reputation Management

Let's briefly review reputation management, as it will provide us with enough information to test the Triple-A rule on the hotel satisfaction score.

Studies from www.reviewpro.com demonstrate that the top three reasons why a guest selects a hotel are:
- Guest experience factors (i.e. guest reviews and satisfaction scores)
- Location
- Price

With this in mind, it is easy to understand why the guest experience factor plays such a big role in the ranking algorithms of various websites. It also explains why reputation management is becoming increasingly important and is an accurate predictor of a hotel's performance.

Do you know what your guests are saying about your hotel? Do you reply to online reviews? What is your online reputation?

We can all agree that a high hotel satisfaction score and positive reviews are important, but we also know that it is very time-consuming to read and reply to online reviews.

Luckily, there are many systems out there that can gather all this review data for you. These systems can generate important KPIs and even competitive comparisons, which can help you determine the correct value of your product. Such measurements can also help you understand how to best price yourself in the market. Most systems even allow you to dive deeper into the data to see which departments currently drive negative feedback. You can then quickly identify the source of negative feedback and set up the actions necessary to make improvements.

The ability to read and reply to online reviews and comments on social media through a simple user interface is another key feature and one of the main reasons for investing in a good reputation management system in the first place. Moreover, with a good Rep system, you can also drill down to see what aspect or which department is underperforming.

Reputation management is where hotel operation meets revenue management and where accurate insights can lead to increased hotel guest satisfaction and profitability. I think of guest satisfaction scores or reputation management as digital value units. This is because an online hotel satisfaction score and reputation are equal to the perceived value of a hotel. Travelers view them as strong indicators of whether or not they should select a hotel, thus making them good gauges to determine how much the hotel can charge for a room in comparison to what their competitors charge. We'll take a closer look at this in the next chapter when we discuss value pricing.

For now, let's test the Triple-A rule on the Hotel Satisfaction Score.

Is it Actionable? Yes, very. With a good system, you can drill down to see which department is underperforming. You can, then, on a daily basis, check and measure the exact result of your actions.

Is it Accessible? Yes, definitely. But you have to invest in a good system to make it accessible.

Is it Auditable? Yes. The data is based on the direct feedback of guests, online reviews, and other interactions. This kind of data is very clean and reliable.

Pickup

Pickup statistics can be a good indicator of hotel performance, which is why you should be analyzing them. We will discuss pickup statistics more in the next chapter, but for now, let's look at a short overview of pickup and see if it passes the Triple-A test.

There are several factors to consider when you look at pickup numbers, but first of all: What is a pickup number? When you look at the pickup, you are, for example, going over the reservations you sold the day before. If you look at the current month, you could check pickup day by day to determine rate changes. You could also use the pickup data to figure out if you need to set up restrictions to avoid days filling up too quickly, which might cause surrounding days to be blocked for guests who want to stay many nights.

So, does pickup pass the Triple-A test?

Is it Actionable? Yes, very. Normally it gives you a very good indication of which days you need to take action on. Sometimes you will need to dig a bit deeper to figure out exactly what type of segments were booked to determine the right strategy to follow moving forward, but nonetheless it's actionable.

Also, if you have a system that can compare how much you sold this year versus the previous year, you will have a good indication of whether your hotel is performing well or not.

Is it Accessible? It should be. If you have a decent PMS or revenue management system, you should be able to easily pick out these numbers. Otherwise, a simple excel spreadsheet on which you deduct yesterday's reservation overview from today's will suffice.

Is it Auditable? Yes, it is. The numbers come directly from the PMS or CRS. As long as the basic structures behind the scenes are in place, the number should be highly reliable.

Pace

Looking at the booking pace provides you with a very good indication of whether a certain time period in the future will perform well for your hotel. The pace tells you if you are in line with the same point in time from the previous year or, if you get more advanced, if you are where you need to be to reach the goals you set for a specific period.

If your hotel has a diverse business mix, it's important to understand the different booking windows per segment or rate class. The booking pace is your helper to find opportunities at the right point in time. Since all segments behave differently and the booking windows can vary widely, understanding and working with booking pace can be crucial for taking action before a window closes.

Pace and pickup will be discussed more in the coming chapters. But first, does booking pace pass the Triple-A test?

Is it Actionable? Yes, it is. The booking pace provides you with a very clear indication of whether you are moving in the right direction.

Is it Accessible? Yes, but it depends, of course, on whether you have a good business intelligence system or RMS system in place. If not, at the very least, you should be able to pull the data from your PMS and arrange it in a spreadsheet.

Is it Auditable? Same as for pickup: Yes, it is. The numbers come directly from the PMS or CRS. As long as the basic structures behind the scenes are in place, the number should be highly reliable.

TWO
Learn the Basics

Let's review some of the basics you need to know as a revenue manager and the concepts which are good to know before we dive deeper later in this book.

OCC, ADR, and REVPAR

OCC (or Occupancy) is the percentage or number of sold rooms based on your total inventory. See example in the image below.

ADR (or Average Daily Rate) is the average rate per sold rooms.

RevPAR (or Revenue Per Available Room) is the average rate per room based on your total inventory (e.g. €120 per night x 90% occupancy rate = €90.00). It is worth noting that RevPAR does not measure profitability. Thus, growth in RevPAR doesn't necessarily mean that a hotel's profits are increasing. As a result, revenue managers often use ADR as their main source for measuring performance. ADR has been found to be one of the main factors in OCC, so if a revenue manager prices their rooms appropriately, both the occupancy rate and the RevPAR should increase.

	OCC HOTEL OCCUPANCY %	**ADR** AVERAGE DAILY ROOM RATE	**REVPAR** REVENUE PER AVAILABLE ROOM
CALCULATION	SOLD ROOMS / HOTEL CAPACITY	ROOM REVENUE / SOLD ROOMS	ROOM REVENUE / HOTEL CAPACITY
EXAMPLE	95 SOLD ROOMS / 100 ROOMS TO SELL = 95% OCC	17 325 EURO ROOM REVENUE / 95 SOLD ROOMS = 182 EURO IN ADR	17 325 EURO ROOM REVENUE / 100 ROOMS TO SELL = 173 EURO IN REVPAR

Segmentation

Segmentation is all about putting similar reservations into the same basket.

Why do we want to do that? From a revenue management point of view, we want to segment reservations to be able to gain actionable insights, but you will often have to drill deeper than traditional segmentation to find what you are looking for (more about this later in the book).

From a sales and marketing perspective, segments are very useful since you prefer to talk about people, which is more tangible compared to channels and rate categories.

Having segments that are easy for anyone to understand is crucial since this will be your tool to communicate your work to the rest of the management group and hotel personnel. Having segments is therefore very useful when, for example, planning your budget, forecasting, or presenting in a revenue meeting.

As a revenue manager, it's very handy to use segments when planning for budgets and when forecasting future demand. The reason for this is that you will be able to communicate your actions with easy-to-understand segments.

Traditional segmentation is usually divided into macro and micro segments where each macro segment contains a grouping of minor segments.

Here's an (oversimplified) example of how segmentation could look in a hotel (Macro segment in bold).

TRANSIENTS
> OTA
> WEB
> GDS
> PROMOS

NEGOTIATED
> FIT
> CORPORATE FIXED RATES
> CORPORATE DYNAMIC RATES

GROUPS
    LEISURE GROUPS
    BUSINESS GROUPS
    CONFERENCE GROUPS

Apart from segments, reservations are also usually marked with channels and rate categories.

Channels indicate from which channel the reservations came through. Some examples of distribution channels: Booking.com, OWN website, GDS, etc.

Rate Category is the grouping of similar rate codes. For example, retail, discount, negotiated, blocks, series, qualified, etc.

Please note that segments, channels, and rate categories come in different shapes and names depending on which system you use. Above is a simplified example based on my own experience from working with different systems and company cultures.

Hotel Performance indicators and Benchmarking

Benchmarking your hotel's performance toward your competitors and market is common practice, and for most hotels worldwide, these benchmarks often act as KPIs with which the hotel is measured and used as target indicators for future performance. As mentioned earlier, KPIs such as RevPAR are not informative enough to draw actionable insights from, but it's a good indicator to dig further. The most common system used for benchmarking globally is STR (Smith Travel Research).

Working with benchmarking will help you understand how much potential for growth your hotel has during similar periods from year to year. Did you reach your fair share of the market last year? Did you capture your fair share yesterday? Which days of the week underperform? Where do you have the best chances to grow?

See image below for instructions on how the different benchmarking indexes are calculated. If you, for example, have 0.9 in MPI for last month, it means you have 90% of your fair share. You are missing 10% to capture your fair share of the pie. And since the index is based on the hotel's capacity, it gives a fair indicator and you are not punished if your hotel has more or less rooms to sell compared with other hotels.

MARKET PENETRATION INDEX (MPI)
Market penetration index shows share of room nights sold above or below the average sold in the market

$$\frac{\text{HOTEL'S OCCUPANCY \%}}{\text{MARKET'S OCCUPANCY \%}}$$

AVERAGE RATE INDEX (ARI)
Average rate index shows hotel's average rate position above or below the market average rate

$$\frac{\text{HOTEL'S ARR}}{\text{MARKET'S ARR}}$$

REVENUE GENERATING INDEX (RGI)
Also known as RevPAR index (or penetration...) Revenue generating index shows hotel's share of room revenue above or below the market average

$$\frac{\text{HOTEL'S RevPAR}}{\text{MARKET'S RevPAR}}$$

BAR structure

The BAR (or Best Available Rate) is the lowest unqualified rate for a room type available to the general public. BAR provides a guarantee that guests will not find a lower rate for the same room type on a given night(s) on an OTA (or Online Travel Agent) or elsewhere. This is also a common rate used for rate comparisons between hotels.

I have found that the best way to optimize the BAR structure is to focus your efforts on the BAR levels that stand for 80% of your BAR traffic.

This is a great exercise to figure out what your "real" value is.

Let us say you have 10 BAR levels. See which of these levels bring you the most business at the moment; you should experiment by adding new levels or changing existing ones.

One important thing to remember is to also consider updating BAR to outside the 80% top business, but only the high ones. This might sound counterintuitive, but this is because many times you would have discounts connected to your BAR. When a discount is applied to a higher BAR, the final price for your consumer might be within the 80% span anyway.

Once you figure out what price points are selling the most, you'll also know where you should focus your efforts to make any necessary changes. By targeting the right price points, we can stimulate even more demand in the area that the crowd decided was your actual value.

In the figure below, we can see that 70% of all business is between price point 800 and price point 1,400. The most interesting part is that these price points come from only 30% of all the available price points illustrated in the graph. The second rectangle is also very important because the rates it represents are directly connected to that 70% of all business, since these price points are driving business for lower price points when discounted. In total, we see that 25% to 30% of all the price points represent 80% of the business in this example. If this were your hotel, it is here you would focus your attention.

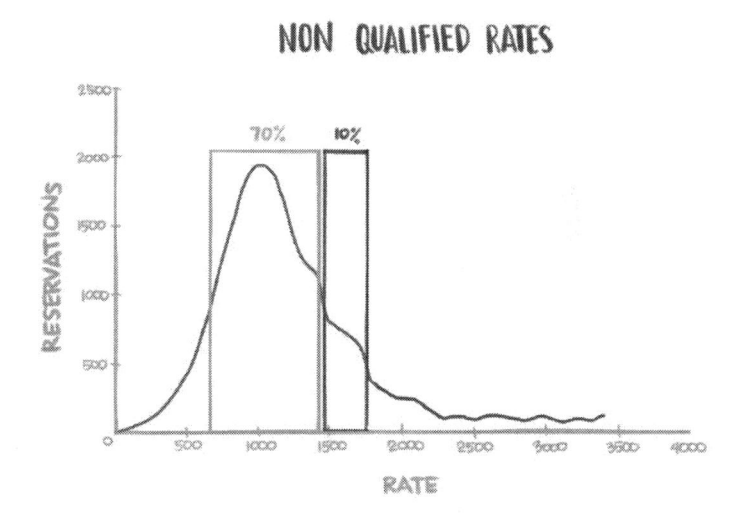

NON QUALIFIED RATES

Create a scatter graph of price points for the business your hotel generates using the data on reservations that you downloaded from your system. If you do not know how to make a scatter graph, just Google it or go to YouTube and watch some videos, and you will become a master at graphing in no time.

This approach will help you gain insight as to where you should focus your efforts to create as much value as possible from your BAR structure.

Another great BAR exercise to do is to make sure your supplements make sense. How much extra do you add for double occupancy, families, etc.? Make sure your rates make sense compared with your competitors and the market.

Flexible and nonrefundable BAR
Most hotels offer two types of BAR. Flexible rates typically mean that the reservation can be changed or cancelled until the day before arrival or sometimes until the same day as arrival. The other BAR type is a discount alternative where the customer must prepay. Reservations made with this rate type cannot be changed or cancelled. Thus, if a guest is willing to book early and commit to the reservation, some money can be saved. This means money in the bank for the hotel and a guarantee that the guest will arrive. Win-win for both parties.

One example of a successful nonrefundable setup is one where the hotel offers different levels of discount depending on how far in advance the guest is willing to book. This creates great search result relevance for hotels and at the same time more reservations long before arrival. It also gives a revenue manager extra tools to optimize the hotel revenue for the last remaining rooms because the base is already there.

Another advantage to catching early bookers is that they have a tendency to spend more money at the hotel since the memory of the purchase is further away when they arrive at the hotel than it is for somebody who booked a couple of days before arrival. In other words, this provides great prospects for upsell at arrival.

Online content

This one is by far one of the most important steps, which also should be reviewed on a regular basis. Making sure online content is up-to-date may fall under marketing in your hotel, but nonetheless, this is one of the most revenue-driving factors you can manage.

By online content, I refer to images, texts, room type descriptions, videos, etc. in all sales channels. If you don't have good content to use, then I suggest hiring a professional photographer to capture some great shots of your property. Rooms, public areas, lobby, facade, spa, gym … all there is. It's worth the investment many, many times over.

I have applied this tactic in multiple properties with poor online content and the result is unbelievable. You will have to invest time in this but once it's up and running, you will reap the rewards at a fast pace.

Now you might ask yourself which channels I refer to. Here's a short cheat sheet:
OTAs (Booking.com, Hotels.com etc…)

GDS
Your own hotel website
FIT/Wholesale
Other channels such as deal sites.

For some channels such as GDS, they normally collect your images from a central image data bank. Figure out where this is and make sure that the image data bank is up-to-date.

It's said that content is king, but if that's true, then context must be God. Make sure your content is persuasive and relevant. We have very little time to persuade the customer to choose our hotels over a competitor's.

A <u>Microsoft study</u> from 2014 shows that the human attention span has fallen from twelve seconds to eight seconds from the year 2000 — around the time the mobile revolution began — to 2014. The attention span of a goldfish is about nine seconds. You have about three to five seconds to make an impression online.

With this in mind, consider how your hotel is displayed in these channels. Studies from www.reviewpro.com show that the top three reasons why a guest selects a hotel are:

1. Guest Experience Factors (i.e. guest reviews and satisfaction scores)
2. Location

3. Price

Do your landing pages and sell screens reflect these three reasons enough? Are they persuasive enough to convince potential guests to book rooms in your hotel? We have to play with the pictures in their heads, not simply what we think will work.

Use your own customer reputation tool or go to www.trustyou.com and search for your hotel. See what your guests place the most value upon. You cannot build on your weakness; you can only build on strength. Do your guests often give you praise for your great breakfast, your great location, or how perfect your hotel is for couples? Make sure to include such strengths in your content on all your major channels. This is a great way to attract the perfect-fit guest for your hotel. Make sure the content is 100% optimized on all your different landing pages with them in mind.

Hotel Images

Make sure you have high-resolution images on all websites. This will optimize your hotel to be responsive for all sorts of devices, from PC to iPad. Make sure you have professional images; your hotel will stand out from the crowd and you will convert higher. We also know that hotel image quality and quantity are important factors in the ranking algorithms on most websites. You should have at least twenty images. Best practice materials from

Expedia indicate that travelers are 150% more engaged on listings with more than twenty photos. Here are some other interesting statements from the same guide:
- Travelers rank guest room images as the most important images to consider when booking a trip.
- 60% of travelers rank bathroom images as very important.
- Travelers want to be able to visualize where they are going to sleep, shower, and relax after a busy day at work.
- Travelers prefer images that showcase your building in relation to the surrounding community. You can encourage them to imagine activities that are just outside your front door by including such images.
- Travelers look for bright lobbies with seating areas where they can relax or catch up on social media. Remember to showcase the public areas in your hotel.
- Food. How many images of food do you see on social media every single day? Food is social, indulgent, and increasingly inspires travel. Include photos of your restaurant, bar, and room service so guests understand all of the opportunities to eat and drink available to them at your hotel. Be sure to highlight any unique experiences with food your guests will encounter, such as communal dining, access to space where guests can picnic, etc.

Hotel description

Make sure your hotel descriptions are up-to-date, relevant, and persuasive.

Did anything change at your hotel? Make sure you display the latest information on all websites.

Hotel descriptions are a great way to attract the perfect-fit guest for your hotel. Make sure the content is 100% optimized on all your different landing pages with them in mind.
Also, make sure to have great room descriptions highlighting the key feature of each room type. Did you remember to tick all boxes under room features? If not, you will risk not appearing in some specific filtered searches.

Demand Calendar

Create a demand calendar for the entire calendar year. Identify potential demand using historical data, large group reservations, and upcoming events.

There are some great tools out there to help you either collect data or provide you with an up-to-date demand calendar. One example is OTA Insight, where you can keep track of the market and your competitors' rate setting as it evolves over time. They also provide information on market demand and upcoming events. If you combine this with your own data, it's a killer tool. Make sure it's up-to-date or it won't be much use to you.

It can be very beneficial for your colleagues to get an updated demand calendar. This will help them make the right decisions when receiving, for example, group requests or phone calls in the evening when you are not there.

If you manage to spot big trends or events in time, you will be able to yield your revenues in time to profit. You will probably find that if you manage to grab five to ten of these high demand dates in time, it's what will make the biggest impact on the bottom line for the hotel.

On a daily basis, you are probably checking 30-60 days out when checking your pickup and pricing, but by having control of 60-365 days out, you get a strong competitive advantage. This is often overseen in hotels without a revenue manager.

Revenue Meetings

This is one of the most important steps. **The key to success is to make sure everyone at the hotel is aligned and knows what actions are needed to reach the desired targets**. This is what will give you the momentum to reach levels you would not have reached otherwise.

I suggest having revenue meetings at least once a month. This is the time to share your findings from forecasting and what actions should be derived from those findings, as well as who to assign ownership for these actions. Revenue meetings are also a good time to reflect on the past period and what learning you can gain from that. For example, did you reach your target? Why or why not? What's the result from the previous actions set and how did those influence new forecasts? We will return back to forecasting later in this book.

Storytelling

"Good stories always beat good spreadsheets."
Chris Sacca -
Early stage investor in companies such as Twitter, Uber, Instagram, Kickstarter, and Twilio.

Something you will learn quickly is that most people won't buy or understand your ideas if you only present them with data in the form of spreadsheets or other "raw data" types. Take revenue meetings as a good example. This is the time to present your ideas and findings from, for example, your latest revenue forecast. If you want everyone on board with your message, you must give your data a soul.

You need to be able to turn your data into stories. Most people aren't the analyst type and you need to be able to convey your message in words and sometimes charts. To be able to get your message across to the rest of the team, you must be able to sell your ideas and discoveries. How do you do that? Same as selling, you tell stories.

Some good ways to do this is to use easy-to-understand charts without too many details. Combine that with market segments or channels to give good relevancy and to convert it to a story. This might sound obvious, but I have seen a lot of good revenue managers not being able to turn their good insight into actionable insights because they forgot this simple rule: give your data a soul. This skill doesn't always come natural to an analytical person, but with enough practice, this skill will make a huge difference in your carrier.

Trendspotting

Be the first to know when there is a new event in town or if one of your competitors will close down for renovation.

Take some time to figure out which newsletters and websites are relevant for your destination. They might include various topics such as conference listing, congress organizers, concerts, sport events, and general industry news.

If you work with a BI system such as OTA Insight, they have much of this data consolidated already to give a good helicopter view of the market.

THREE
Pricing and Optimization

The next step is to understand daily price and inventory optimization tactics.

The decisions you must make regarding daily pricing vary significantly from day to day. It can be rather daunting to know where to begin. Here are some tactics I rely upon over and over again to help me make my decisions.

My successful formula for price and restriction yielding is very simple and goes like this:
Your own pickup trends + inventory control + competitive activities = optimal yield.

Before having a look at what your compset is doing, check your own pickup. Competitive activities are very important but your own pickup is more important.

So before simply following the rate setting of your competitors, have a look at your own "where to play" strategy and why you had these rates and restrictions in the first place.

Pickup trends

Do not adjust your pricing and restrictions based on the pickup number. We need to know what is driving the pickup in order to see if we need to make any adjustments.

Ask yourself, what was booked yesterday? How did it affect the business we already had?

You might want to think twice before raising your rate if you know that you only had pickup in segments with static rates. In this situation, raising your dynamic rates might depress the pickup on your higher yielding rates, including these dynamic rates.

Is your pickup filling up too quickly from lower-paying segments? If so, consider setting up some restrictions. Different alternatives here can be to either close lower-paying segments completely or restrict availability with MLOS or CTA.

MLOS = Minimum Length of Stay. Set a limit to how many nights minimum somebody has to stay to be able to book the specific rate or room type

CTA = Closed to Arrival. Close the day for arrival in lower-paying segments. You can only stay this day if your arrival day is another day prior to this one.

If you are not using a revenue management system, the best way to set restrictions is by rate category and room types. As discussed in the first chapter of this course, the rate category structure was designed for this purpose.

A couple of times a week you should probably ask yourself what will be going on four to twelve months into the future. In particular, while looking ahead, try to identify new trends or trends that are repeating themselves.

Market and Competitors

It is also important to keep an eye on what your competitors are doing. Watching your competitors will let you know when good opportunities exist to increase rates and help you identify trends before you might have otherwise. If you don't already have a tool to track this kind of information, the major OTAs, at the very least, offer free tools, which is better than nothing. Rate Intelligence from Booking.com is just one example.

I have tested many different tools for competitive rate intelligence, and the best one I have encountered so far is OTA Insight (www.otainsight.com). This site offers a very simple tool with a clean user interface. It also provides very accurate demand forecasts for the near future. I always say, once you find a tool that even a general manager likes and wants to use, then you know you've found the right one. OTA Insight is the first such tool I have found that matches this criterion.

Add surveillance for certain areas to make sure you are prepared once that area is filled up.

Inventory Control

Make sure your room inventory is always balanced.

In other words, make sure you have rooms available when they need to be available. If you sold out of your most popular room type, you might want to upgrade or set up overbooking rules in order to not miss out on good opportunities such as long stayers and last-minute premium rate bookers.

If, for example, your standard room category sells out for a Tuesday, you might miss out on guests who have agreements only for that particular room type, but who want to stay several nights in addition to Tuesday.

Here is an example of an availability overview. For April 12, we can see that all standard rooms are sold out, but we have plenty of availability in the superior and deluxe category.

This problem presents us with a great opportunity to increase room inventory for standard rooms. However, we should not repeat the same scenario again and risk only selling standard rooms for one night on April 12. Therefore, we must also set up restrictions to be able to fence out reservations that will only stay for one night. Obviously, there are more aspects to consider in different scenarios, but this is an oversimplified example and the solution presents a general framework for dealing with similar situations.

	Standard Room	Superior Room	Deluxe Room	Suite	Total
06-apr	10	15	6	2	33
07-apr	34	30	8	2	74
08-apr	23	25	10	2	60
09-apr	36	23	10	2	71
10-apr	35	24	13	2	74
11-apr	35	27	10	1	73
12-apr	-3	25	12	2	36
13-apr	33	22	9	2	66
14-apr	28	23	10	2	63
15-apr	27	26	12	0	65
16-apr	30	25	10	2	67
17-apr	23	23	7	2	55
18-apr	33	24	7	2	66

Another great suggestion is to make sure your transactions deliver enough value. We sometimes find that the demand in a city is higher than its supply of hotel rooms. We all have the temptation, then, to price our rooms just a little bit higher than normal — especially by pushing our highest rate higher than we normally would. We must still consider this decision wisely before making such a decision to raise prices.

We must understand the value of our product; otherwise, we will risk having guests leaving the hotel thinking, "Well, I had to find a room in the city even if rates were high, but I definitely didn't receive enough value from the price I paid for it." They will leave the hotel feeling that they paid a high price only because they had to get a room in the city regardless. The guest will not feel, however, that they actually paid a price equivalent to the value of the product they received. This "feeling" of theirs can return to haunt your hotel in various ways, including such guests writing negative reviews (especially regarding value-for-price), being unwilling to promote your hotel to others, and, of course, choosing to lodge elsewhere in the future.

Another thing to consider about charging a price that is too high compared with the actual value of the product received is that when guests pay a price they believe to be too high, even before arriving at your hotel, they tend to look for evidence that confirms their belief that they are not getting the worth they paid a premium for. They will use this evidence against you, either in the form of complaints or negative reviews. On the opposite side of this equation, however, is that if you sell your rooms at a price point that matches the correct value of your product, you will turn this "tendency" around: guests will look for evidence that confirms their belief that they received great value for their money.

We cannot just make our decisions from a logical revenue manager's standpoint; we must also consider and understand the psychological standpoint of the other human beings partaking in these transactions. In the next chapter we will continue the discussion around value-based pricing.

Create your own booking curve

What is a booking curve? A tool that can visually represent bookings over time, incorporating data such as pickup, number of bookings, availability, and yielding capacity of the hotel.

Sound complicated? To make it simpler, a booking curve can help you visualize your current booking status and give you a good indication if you are ahead or behind where you have to be. It is not only extremely useful for pricing but also for many more purposes.

Here are some more examples:

- Staffing
- Room and rate forecasting
- Deep analysis (for example, identifying when specific segments book)

The following graph visualizes how the rooms fill up over time and how this year compares with last year. I have also included the supporting data. The booking curve displays the reservation status for June 10, 2016. In this example, the hotel has 100 rooms and it is 12 days until arrival.

THE BOOKING CURVE

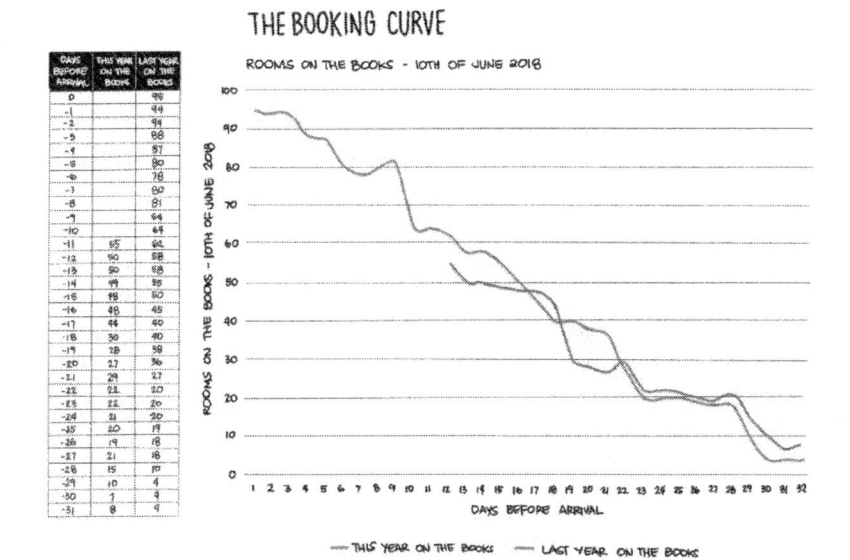

ROOMS ON THE BOOKS - 10TH OF JUNE 2018

DAYS BEFORE ARRIVAL	THIS YEAR ON THE BOOKS	LAST YEAR ON THE BOOKS
0		98
-1		94
-2		94
-3		88
-4		87
-5		80
-6		78
-7		80
-8		81
-9		64
-10		64
-11	65	62
-12	90	58
-13	50	58
-14	49	55
-15	49	50
-16	48	45
-17	44	40
-18	30	40
-19	28	38
-20	27	36
-21	29	27
-22	22	20
-23	22	20
-24	21	20
-25	20	19
-26	19	18
-27	21	18
-28	15	10
-29	10	4
-30	7	4
-31	8	4

—— THIS YEAR ON THE BOOKS   —— LAST YEAR ON THE BOOKS

RM Automation

More and more revenue management systems are being developed that can help you to either semi-automate or fully automate pricing activities. This is fantastic because it will give you more space to focus on the high-value tasks such as forecasting, improving your perceived value, and reputation management.

But do not fall into the trap believing that you will become the master over some super smart AI agent which will do all the grinding for you. Perhaps somewhere in the future this will be possible, but if that was the case anytime in the next 10-20 years, you would not be reading this book right now.

Automation has come a long way in the last 10 years but it's my strong conviction that it's merely a way for you to gain superpowers. Man and machine working together where you — the revenue analyst — are the manager who reacts at all the actionable insights gained from the system.

If you work with a RM system that claims it can automate your daily pricing activities, you are the master who has to feed it with relevant data. It comes back to the first principle of data. Shit in, shit out.

A system which is managed properly will, however, provide you with the power to optimize the time you spend setting prices and give you the power to do it more efficiently than you could without it. Best of all it would give you more time to pursue other valuable tasks.

In his book *Zero to One*, Peter Thiel (co-founder of PayPal) tells a similar story of how they came to this similar realisation.

In the mid-2000s, when they were processing hundreds or even thousands of transactions per second, they were losing upwards of 10 million USD to credit card fraud every month. They couldn't possibly review every single transaction to find the fraud in time to stop it.

To solve the problem, they used a team of highly skilled mathematicians to study fraudulent transfer. They took what they learned and created a software to automatically identify and cancel transactions in real time.

The only problem was that after an hour or two, these imposters would catch on and change their tactics. They were dealing with an adaptive enemy and their software couldn't adapt in response.

The imposters were able to fool the software, but they noticed that they didn't fool the human analysts as easily.

This led to the hybrid model where the computer would flag the most suspicious transactions using a well-designed user interface, and a human operator would make the final judgment to their legitimacy.

Thanks to this hybrid approach, they managed to turn this trend around and profit at a massive scale. The rest is history.

I think this is a great example of how I believe a revenue manager should work. Make sure you become that person who is flagged with relevant information to take action on.

FOUR
Value

"Digital value is probably the most accurate indicator for pricing your hotel."

Johan Hammer

In the classic book *Influence* by Robert Cialdini, the author says that advertisers love to inform us when a product is the "fastest-growing" or "largest-selling" because, by doing so, they don't have to convince us directly that the product is good; they need only say that many others think so, which seems proof enough.

This human tendency is often referred to as the social proof tendency and can be translated simply as: "What other people think influences what we think."

Robert Cialdini continues by saying that 95% of people are imitators and only 5% are initiators; people are persuaded more by the actions of others than by any proof we can offer.

Another human tendency which marketers tend to play around with a lot is the scarcity tendency. We have all experienced this one. For example, at OTA websites, it could say things like "Two rooms left in this category," "Ten people are looking at this hotel right now," or "Popular hotel."

The scarcity tendency tricks us into believing that things or opportunities are more valuable to us when their availability is limited.

On the topic of scarcity, Robert Cialdini writes that "the idea of a potential loss plays a large role in human decision-making. In fact, people seem to be more motivated by the thought of losing something than by the thought of gaining something of equal value."

What happens when marketers combine these two tendencies or even more tendencies? Well, that's persuasion at the highest level.

When we look to book accommodation somewhere, we often search multiple sites for information. By using Google, Booking.com, or a hotel's own website, we typically narrow down our options to a couple of potential hotels. When doing so, we may have even been influenced by the abovementioned tendencies.

For our final selection, we tend to consciously or subconsciously look at the overall value. But how do we determine which hotel is most valuable to us?

We use factors such as location, price, review score, and reviews to determine which hotel has the best value. If a hotel is priced too high compared with the perceived value, it's very likely that we will select something else. If a hotel is priced well in comparison to the perceived value, we are more likely to make a reservation. So if the perceived value is high, the hotel get better placement, more reviews, more visitors on their website, more direct bookings, and, ultimately, more revenue.

Working actively with reputation management is a great way to improve your perceived digital value. This includes responding to reviews in various channels, identifying where you can improve, and following up on previously set goals.

There are many good tools to manage online reputation such as Revinate and ReviewPro. To read more about reputation management please revisit page 18 in this book.

Value Pricing

We can also refer to value pricing as your perceived online value. This is the value that the online consumer or shopper equates with your hotel.

Parameters to help you measure your perceived value are, for example, guest satisfaction score, likes, management responses, and the number of reviews your hotel receives.

The concept of value pricing is to optimize your pricing in relation to how your potential guests perceive your value compared with your competitor's value or with the market.

It's no secret that hotels with high satisfaction scores get more reservations, but it's easy to forget that it can also be a good pricing indicator. If your hotel delivers higher value than your competitors, you should be able to price your hotel higher.

Other aspects that help to improve your perceived value are good placement on various booking websites and good hotel content, images, videos, and text. As you well know, good content and favorable review scores help you rank higher on various websites such as Booking.com and Expedia.

With this in mind, it's easy to see how an increased review score can be converted into digital value units since it's directly correlated to your being able to offer higher prices. If you offer increased value compared with your competitors, you should be able to price accordingly.

A 2013 study from Cornell University shows that hotels with a higher review score are able to sell rooms at higher rates and still retain occupancy levels. In fact, hotels are able to increase rates more than 5% if they increase their review score by one point on a scale from one to ten.

Calculate your price value

A simple way to give you an idea if your price is in line with your value is to convert it into a value index.

Firstly, you have to convert rate and review score into similar numerical units.

For example, let's say that you compare yourself with five other hotels in the market (similar hotels).

Price
Your price 850 Euro
Average competitor price 875 Euro
Calculate 850 / 875 = **0.97**

Review score
Your review score 8.6 / 10
Average competitor review score 8.4 / 10
Calculate 8.6 / 8.4 = **1.02**

Now let's combine it to determine price value
0.97 (price) / 1.02 (review) = 0.95

In this case, your index is 0.95 which could indicate that you are underpricing your hotel. This could also very well be used as a strategy considering that pricing your hotel lower than the actual value would give your hotel great price value when online consumers compare your hotel with your competitors. Obviously there could be other factors to consider but this is a simple exercise to examine your price value. Looking at this index on a day-to-day basis is probably not the best way to use it. Instead I suggest using it for longer time periods such as weeks or months or perhaps during special events in the destination.

The billboard effect

The billboard effect suggests that the more eyeballs you can attract, the more bookings you get. This sounds kind of obvious. Basic marketing, right?

There's a twist to it. A study by Sabrina Lugo at Ice Portal (www.iceportal.com) suggests that up to 50% of customers visit a hotel website after seeing the hotel at an OTA.

WIHP (or World Independent Hotels Promotion) also conducted a study on the billboard effect. What they found was that over 20% of bookings on a hotel's website occurred after that guest found the hotel on an OTA. So not only can an OTA increase bookings through external sites, an OTA can even increase direct bookings from the hotel's own website.

The billboard effect suggests that you should treat your OTA profiles and social media profiles like an extension of your own website.
Once you get them to your website, that's when you need to grab them (if you prefer direct bookings). :)

Make sure to improve your digital value to get high on the list if you want more direct bookings.

Here follows some useful tricks to improve your digital value:

- Set clear goals you can follow up on.
- Identify bottlenecks. What is usually something customers complain about?
- Set a price value strategy. Which price value score is optimal for your hotel and how do you follow up on it on a regular basis?
- Involve everyone at the hotel. Improving value comes down to providing great service experiences at the hotel. Make sure everyone understands your strategy and make sure to keep everyone in the feedback loop.
- Activate the silent mass. It's usually the happiest and the most disappointed guests who write reviews. The majority of people are, however, the ones who enjoyed the stay but weren't thrilled enough to give a review. Figure out how to activate this silent mass. This should eventually raise your overall review score. If you use a reputation management tool, ask them for ways to do this. They are the experts in that area.
- Improve your online content (see page 34 for more tips and tricks).

FIVE

Rocket Science and Wishful Thinking

"I think wishful thinking is innate in the human brain. You want things to be the way you wish them to be, and so you tend to filter information that you shouldn't filter."
Elon Musk

Forecasting and optimizing future demand is probably the most challenging and important task you have as a revenue manager.

One might think it's the technical and analytical part that is the most challenging, but it's more about overcoming psychological barriers which prevent you from even reaching that stage of the exercise.

It's often in the initial stages of forecasting that we get stuck, simply because we tend to explain or dismiss uncertainty and unpredicted projections based on our gut feeling or intuition.

Here's a simple test to illustrate the point I am trying to make.

If a bat and a baseball cost $1.10 together, and the bat costs $1 more than the ball, how much does the ball cost?

What was your answer? If you answered based on your gut feeling, then "ten cents" most likely is your answer. You didn't spend a lot of time on the question and you didn't sit down to calculate it out. "Ten cents" just felt right. However, you, just like almost everybody who reads this famous question, are wrong.

This question is part of the Cognitive Reflection Test, which has shown that most people answer on what feels right rather than truly reflecting on the question. They read this question and immediately conclude that it has to be "ten cents," without ever carefully considering the question. As a result, they never realize their mistake, let alone come up with the right answer (the ball costs five cents). This is completely normal behavior. We tend to go with our gut feelings.

Strong hunches and gut feeling can still be very useful especially if you have long experience in the field. Nonetheless, when it comes to revenue management, intuition or gut feelings are less accurate. There are simply too many variables to consider and the distribution landscape is changing at a rapid pace. Basing important decisions on gut feeling alone is a very risky move.

A combination of experience and data-driven decision-making is the winning formula. Until you have enough experience, go for the latter.

It's your job as a revenue manager to not jump to quick conclusions; instead, you should analyse future trends and set new actionable targets.

If your projections show you a negative trend such as a specific segment that is underperforming, it's your job to set necessary actions in place to put you back on target.

Your projections could also display positive trends and sometimes over-positive trends. You might be selling out too quickly and have underestimated the demand for a particular period.

In such a scenario, you would probably need to raise rates or set up restrictions — sometimes also referred to as fencing.

Fencing is when you set up certain rules to make sure certain rate categories or segments (typically highly discounted rates) are restricted. An example would be a minimum length of stay, closed for arrival, or complete close out.

Such rules can be applied directly in different channels, through a channel manager, or directly in your hotel system. Some hotel systems (PMSs) have the ability to set up rules like, if we reach 90% occupancy, then do X. This is a great way to protect yourself in case you miss something important. Spot and react to this in real time.

Okay, back to forecasting. Normally a hotel sets a yearly target or budget. Optimally this is done month by month and by segment or rate category. Yearly targets are typically based on the performance of the previous year, upcoming events which impact the whole market, demographic trends, market shares, and what you have already on the books.

When forecasting, you check to see if the target can still be met and what to do about it.

I often see hotels rely on the forecasts provided by their system, but that's a mistake since the system won't tell you what you have to do to actually reach your target. System generated forecasts should only act as an indication of what will happen if you take a passive role.

Here are three important questions to ask yourself about forecasting:

If your forecast is on target, what do you have to do to stay on target?

If your forecast is below target, what do you have to do to get back to target?

If your forecast is above target, what will the new target be and what do you have to do to reach it?

I call this way of forecasting *action forecasting*.

Action forecasting

This is the best way by far for approaching the challenge of making a good forecast. A combination of historical facts, current trends, ongoing actions, and new actions meld to create a realistic forecast.

Here, we rely upon historical data, ongoing actions, current reservation trends, and new action points to make a projected outcome based on action, not wishful thinking.

I have successfully applied action forecasting for many years, and what follows is a guide for you to do the same.

A hack to start using this approach to forecasting effectively is to understand your lead-time. What kind of business is booked and at what point in time?

Gather data and additional forecasts

Set up a procedure to have the group-booking department and/or conference department create a three- to six-month forecast for all groups. They should provide you with this forecast five to ten days before you create your own forecast. This should not be something big or time-consuming for them to accomplish.

How big are the variations they predict based on their own experience and day-to-day relationship with group bookers? Do they predict that groups will cancel, change the number of rooms booked (either up or down), etc.?

Relying on this procedure to gather more data will create additional benefits. Before you know it, there will no longer be any groups remaining with questions marks! This forecast procedure also ensures that regular follow up with all groups is made.

Lead-time buckets

Let's divide your business into three buckets.
1. Base = for many hotels, this is their most important kind of business. A rule of thumb is that if you have a healthy base, you can yield higher rates for your remaining rooms. Base business is normally lower-paying groups, crew, or transient early birds.

2. Fill up = corporate and other individuals booking fifteen to sixty days before they are scheduled to arrive.
3. Top up = the business you generate zero to fourteen days before arrival. To perform the best, you need to have your base and fill up buckets working effectively.

We will return to this in the next chapter when we discuss booking windows more in depth.

Forecast Periods

The absolute best way is to make forecasts for an entire period both by the month, when it's done far in advance, and daily for the short term.

–30 days or more into the future, make forecasts a minimum of once a month.

–30 days or less, make forecasts every day.

Identify Bottlenecks and over performance

Do not look at the overall performance; you have to dissect your business to see if you are on track with budgeted performance and where it underperforms. You need to be able to answer: what is currently driving your pickup in occupancy for a particular period? Can you do anything to stimulate pickup in poorly performing customer segments or rate categories?

Action

Create actions where you see opportunities. Ask yourself, can I overperform in one segment to help compensate for loss in another?

Be sure to follow up on previous actions created last month. Are they working: yes or no? If not, you must quickly pivot in another direction.

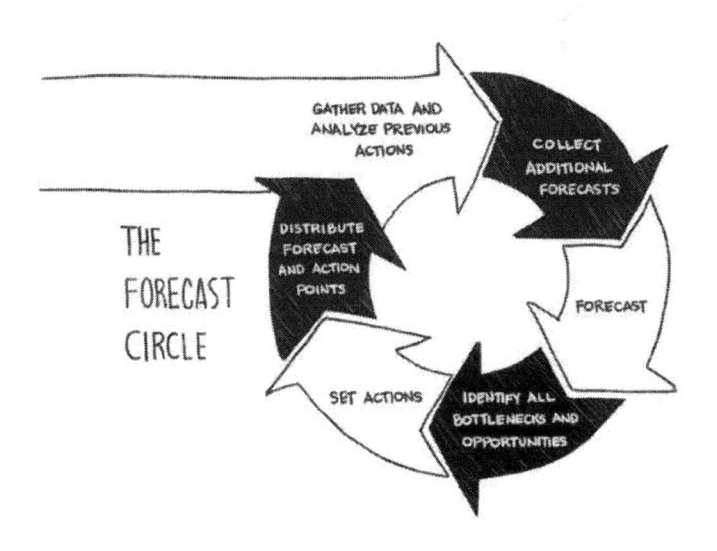

THE FORECAST CIRCLE

- GATHER DATA AND ANALYZE PREVIOUS ACTIONS
- COLLECT ADDITIONAL FORECASTS
- FORECAST
- IDENTIFY ALL BOTTLENECKS AND OPPORTUNITIES
- SET ACTIONS
- DISTRIBUTE FORECAST AND ACTION POINTS

Pace

A good and effective tool to quickly identify what periods in the future need your attention is to compare your booking pace with other similar periods in time, for example, last year. This might seem somewhat abstract in the beginning but once you get the hang of it, you will find it's the most powerful tool for successful action forecasting.

Here's an example of how to convert your pace to a good performance indicator. Think of it as an indicator telling you if you are where you need to be at this point in time to be able to reach your target for some specific period in the future.

Let's say we are looking at how September 2019 is pacing in terms of sold rooms (by pacing I mean how much we have on the books right now compared with, for example, the same point in time last year).

We use the following data:
    a. On The Books
    b. On The Books Last Year (same point in time)
    c. Result Last Year
    d. New Target / Budget

So, in the case of September, how is it pacing? Looks like it is pacing good: +12% where we need to be right now to reach the set targets. +12% sounds great, but is it too great, perhaps? This is just a made up example but pacing high could indicate that you are selling your rooms too fast at perhaps a too low rate. Further analysis is needed to find the cause and set actions accordingly. Likewise, it's probably wise to see what's going on in January and May since it's pacing quite low.

Rooms sold pace for 2019 as of 12th of November 2018. This can likewise be applied to ADR or Total Revenue.

2019

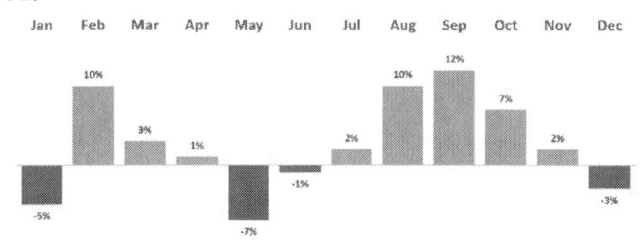

Jan -5%, Feb 10%, Mar 3%, Apr 1%, May -7%, Jun -1%, Jul 2%, Aug 10%, Sep 12%, Oct 7%, Nov 2%, Dec -3%

The formula I use to calculate pace is: (I refer to the letters in the list above)
$((c-b)/c) - ((d-a)/d)$

I want to point out that there are forecasting systems which can give you an even more precise indication of your pace based on many more variables than what we included in this example. This is, however, a good and reliable way to create a pace prediction based on the data you have readily available.

SIX

Booking Windows

A booking window is a certain period prior to the stay date. Here's an example: If you are analysing reservations made for the 14th of January, you can split them up based on how many days prior to that arrival date they were booked. This is also called lead-time or booking lead-time. This is also what is illustrated on a pickup chart.

While looking at the 14th of January, you will be able check how many bookings were made during a specific booking window.

Stay / Business Date - January 14

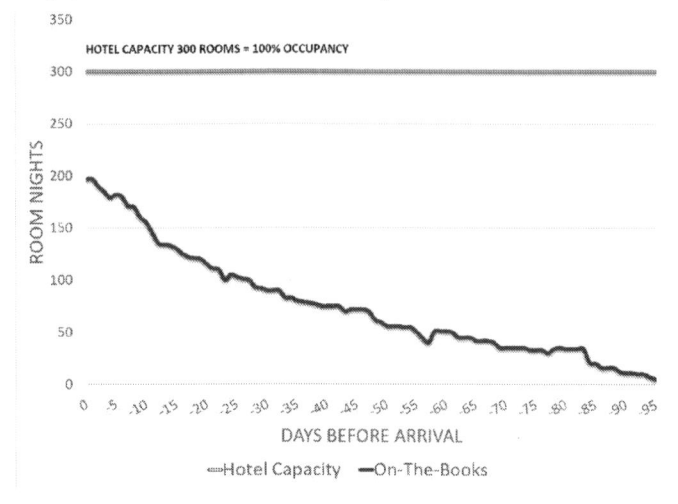

So, why is this important and why did it get its own chapter? :)

Working with booking windows is especially beneficial while forecasting future demand since you can take advantage of historic data to forecast future demand, and more importantly use the knowledge to stimulate new demand in bookings windows where you were previously weak.

"Not all reservations behave the same." Different segments or customer types book your hotels very differently. This is where traditional segments might fail since even within similar customer groups there are distinct separation and even outlier opportunities to take advantage of.

If you learn to understand the booking windows of your hotel, it will provide you with a big competitive advantage.

To illustrate some simple examples: group reservations have to be booked further in advance compared with your corporate travelers, but also within these customer groups there can be a clear separation. Some look for early booking offers whilst some book last minute. Is your hotel relevant within all booking windows for the types of customer you would like to attract?

Being relevant in various booking windows doesn't necessarily mean having the lowest rates. Sometimes this will work, but there's more to it than just lowering rates for dates far out in the future.

When I was working for a large hotel chain, we set out to investigate if we should change how we discount our best available rates depending on when the traveler makes the reservation. This was done simply to reward someone who is committed to making a reservation far in advance. Obviously this also came with the restrictions of having to prepay the entire reservation to claim any good savings.

During the analysis phase, we noticed that we were not very good at attracting transient travelers who were booking 21 days or earlier to arrival. At that time, we only had one type of discount which was valid no matter how far in advance you booked.

Our conclusion was that we didn't have a very attractive offer for someone who booked far in advance. This made us not relevant to travelers during those booking windows and if we were not relevant, we would fall low on all lists as a result of that.

Less exposure on booking sites equals less bookings and less billboard effect.

We set out to change that. The new structure was divided into three different discount levels depending on the booking window. The earlier you booked, the bigger discount you received. We thought: *"Great, more bookings far in advance, money in the bank (prepayments), and better opportunities to yield higher rates in shorter booking windows"*.

It also gave the revenue managers the possibility to close the higher discounts whenever capacity was distressed.

The result was incredible but not in the way we predicted.

We did capture these +21 days booking windows as per our ambitions, but the results were even better than expected. We were sure that customers would book our new discount levels with prepayments but the majority of new demand we captured actually booked non-discounted FLEX rates. Obviously the risk of cancellation was higher but the cancellation ratio value was too low to make an impact compared with these fantastic rates that were booked.

It's hard to know exactly why customers choose to book the higher rates instead of the new discount rates, but my own personal conclusion is that we became relevant in these new booking windows. We were discovered due to our good rates, which led to customers checking images and other content on the landing pages, but in the end they booked a FLEX rate since their travel itinerary wasn't confirmed yet. Our rates made us relevant.

Booking window optimization

Here's an example of how to illustrate booking windows for just one individual stay date for your hotel.

As you can see below, one small action in a booking window can lead to an exponential increase in revenue.

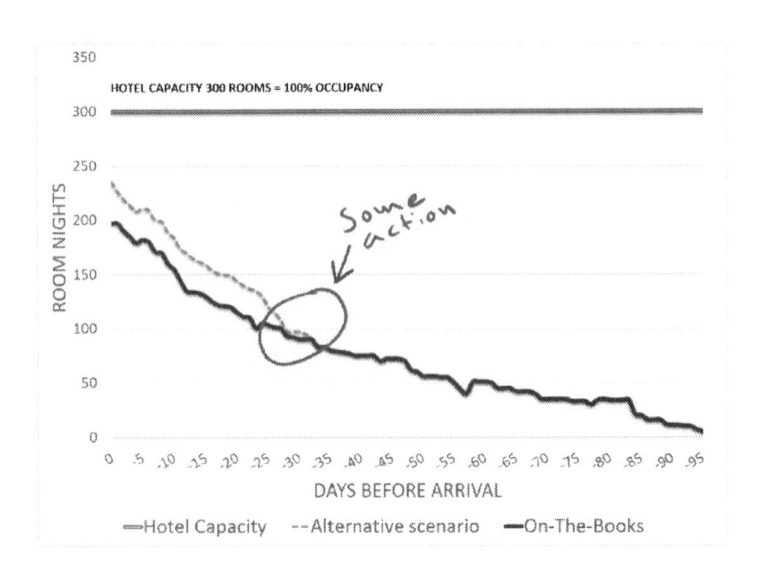

Imagine if that one action you take in booking window 21-30 days before arrival leads to an average daily revenue increase of 300 Euro. If that action affects a full year, it will lead to a yearly result of more than 100 000 Euro. This is more effective than trying to optimize single stay dates.

It can be hard to measure the impact of booking window optimization, but the overall result will speak for itself.

If you react too late because you only look at your prices the week before the actual stay dates, then you lost that window of opportunity to create traction in booking windows that are further out. My advice is to be proactive—always look ahead and optimize your booking windows

Key takeaway:
Booking window optimization is the secret weapon of successful hotel revenue managers. It can be challenging to master and it requires some practice, which is mostly because it's a bit abstract and hidden in plain sight.

The main difference between booking window optimization and only optimizing pricing on a daily basis is that revenue growth due to daily pricing optimization is typically linear while booking window optimization revenue growth is exponential. One does not exclude the other, but focusing on booking windows will give you more return on time invested. See 80/20 rule on page 11.

Booking windows by market

Another beneficial task is to check what specific markets book and how long before arrival they book.

Run a few targeted campaigns. If you do not have access to such information, then ask some of your biggest OTA partners if they can provide you with the information you need. If you know that US travelers with high ADRs typically book eight weeks in advance for the month of June, then perhaps it's wise to target that group even more.

Time Value

The general belief is that customers who book far in advance are people looking for a good early bird deal. We normally start at a lower bar and raise the rate in accordance with the market and a natural pace of new reservations. We do this because the market says we should and our customers expect it, but why? There is more to it than just market behavior. There is also a psychological aspect to it, a very profound one. Humans tend to discount the future. What do I mean by that?

When it comes to experiences—and in our case a service experience—we do not value it as high when it takes place well into the future than we would when purchasing it just a couple a days before.

In other words, we don't want to pay as much for something when we reserve or pay for it far in advance.

In his book *Misbehaving - The Making of Behavioral Economics*, the 2017 Economics Nobel Prize winner, Richard TH. Thaler, argues that "the basic idea is that consumption is worth more to you now than later. If given a choice between a great dinner this week or one a year from now, most of us would prefer the dinner sooner than later." Richard used a formulation called the Samuelson formulation to calculate the "discount" to future consumption. If a dinner a year from now is only considered to be 90% as good as one right now, we are said to be discounting the future at an annual rate of about 10%.

For more in-depth discussions around future discounting and the exciting field of Behavioral Economics, I strongly recommend reading his book.

SEVEN
Group Pricing and Displacement

When it comes to group pricing, there are two different aspects worth discussing. One aspect is displacement or what I like to call the *What If*. The other aspect concerns what constitutes a good rate to offer a group.

A *What If* analysis requires that you determine how much business you must say "No" to if you accept a group. Basically, you need to look at what business you are expecting for the dates in question and whether the group replaces that business. You must also remember to add in extra revenues you would not have had otherwise with, for example, transient guests (conference room rental, food, etc.).

To make these calculations and answer these questions, conduct a *What If* analysis. To do so, you can either look at historical data or forecast performance with these specific dates in mind. Remember, you don't always need to reinvent the wheel when you get a new group request that necessitates making a *What If* analysis. Take time to create a truly practical template that you can use to make this an effortless procedure every single time.

Here's a very simple *What If* exercise example:

Our imaginary hotel has a capacity of 100. In other words, the hotel can sell 100 rooms per day.

Here is the forecast for the hotel for the same period the group wants to stay. The group request is spread over three days and the number of rooms booked peak on the second day.

FORECAST EXCLUDING GROUP	DAY 1	DAY 2	DAY 3	TOTAL
FORECAST HOTEL OCCUPANCY	82%	95%	67%	
FORECAST ROOM NIGHTS	82	95	67	
FORECAST AVERAGE RATE	$167	$189	$174	
TOTAL REVENUE	$13 694	$17 955	$11 658	$43 307

Here is the group request:

GROUP DETAILS	DAY 1	DAY 2	DAY 3
GROUP REQUEST (NUMBER OF ROOMS)	25	30	20
GROUP RATE PER ROOM	$100	$100	$100
GROUP CONFERENCE REVENUE	$500	$650	$500

This is the new forecast if the group is accepted:

NEW FORECAST WITH GROUP	DAY 1	DAY 2	DAY 3	TOTAL
FORECAST HOTEL OCCUPANCY	100%	100%	87%	
FORECAST ROOM NIGHTS	100	100	87	
FORECAST AVERAGE RATE	$150	$162	$157	
TOTAL REVENUE (+ NEW CONFERENCE REVENUE)	$15 525	$16 880	$14 158	$46 563

RESULT	DAY 1	DAY 2	DAY 3	TOTAL
VARIATIONS	$+1 831	$-1 075	$+2 500	$+3 256

Even if the group receives a much lower price per room compared with the forecasted average price per room, the calculation turns out to be a positive. The extra conference revenue is partially to thank for this. In the end, our imaginary hotel earns $3 256 extra by accepting this group. Please note that this is an oversimplified example, which does not consider what reservations are already on the books, the additional operational costs associated with booking the group, and the average length of stay of the displaced room nights.

You can probably see how similar approaches can be applied for evaluating new corporate contracts or re-evaluating historic contracts such as big group tour series, FIT contracts, or corporate contracts.

Group Pricing

When it comes to group pricing, assuming you don't already have an agreed-upon rate with the hotel as a company or with a travel agent, figure out what would be the best rate to offer a group in order to win its business away from your competitors.

One great way to do this is to first look at the groups you did "win" in the past and see what rates you offered them in situations with similar circumstances. For example, let's say in January of last year you received a group request for a June booking. You offered a room rate of one hundred Euros per night and won that business. It might be a good idea, then, if you receive another group request for June in January of this year to offer a similar rate.

It's also very important to look at the lead-time of the request. In this example, a request received in January for a booking in June has a five-month lead-time. However, if you receive the request in May for the June booking—a one-month lead-time—then you probably want to offer a different rate.

When doing this exercise, be sure to factor in lead-time and season. Make a habit of creating documents with this data, which you can easily locate and reference when quoting rates to future groups.

A similar exercise inverts this process, allowing you to evaluate the groups you lost, rather than won. Determine at what rates you lose most groups for different lead times. I strongly suggest that you implement a system where you can—once a year or, preferably, once a month—evaluate all the lost business to see how you can approach rate setting differently in the future.

Demand Calendar for groups

To explain demand calendars a bit more, I further believe it is good to indicate how much base business you would accept per day. By base business I mean groups, but also individuals booking far in advance. Once you define what base business is in your hotel and where you must draw the line for what you consider as base business, identify how much you're willing to accept per day during different seasons.

To perform this exercise, you obviously need to figure out what a healthy level of base business at your hotel looks like. By using historical data and looking at your different group segments, you will be able to determine what your historical levels of base business were and how much you're willing to accept for similar periods in the future. You also need to factor in events that will occur during the new period.

If you have access to systems with competitive intelligence, factor them in as well. This allows you to compare your own on-the-books situation with that of your competitors and/or the market as a whole.

Even if your high seasons are only a couple of months every year, and you don't see the point of creating a demand calendar for the entire year, specifying how much base business you're willing to take is, nevertheless, a great exercise to perform. Once you have a good calendar, it becomes a wonderful tool to pass out to other departments in the hotel, including those headed by the front office manager and reservation manager, so they too can have a nice, simple overview. It also helps other employees to help you, allowing them to make more decisions themselves without their needing to request your constant feedback.

One very important factor you need to consider while making this demand calendar is that you need to know what the wash rate is within different segments. Wash rate means how much of the initial group block did not materialize. For example, if a group blocks 100 rooms but cancels 30 of them within the contracted deadline, the wash rate for that group is 30%.

The wash rates often vary between segments and seasons. Leisure tour groups are more likely to wash than a business group.

Why do you need to know this? This is mainly because you probably want to sell more rooms than you have when you factor in wash rates. As an oversimplified example, if you set your base business contribution to be 30% on a given date and you know you will have at least a 50% wash rate, you should probably accept groups or other base business at a rate of up to 50 or 60%.

EIGHT
More Optimization

In this chapter we will discuss some tactics when it comes to optimizing your distribution channels. We'll look at direct booking optimization, some best practices for campaigns and promotions, and general product distribution.

Get more direct bookings

I will not go into details on how to drive more direct traffic; instead, we will focus on how to make sure the traffic converts to a booking. I chose to not discuss the challenge of driving more traffic simply because it doesn't qualify as a timeless principle in this book. In chapter four, we have already seen how, for example, the billboard effect can give more traffic, but converting traffic to bookings qualifies better as a timeless principle. I believe designing your website for different kinds of customer journeys is key to converting higher.

Think of your hotel website as your digital reception desk and that your traffic is potential customers walking into your virtual lobby. With this analogy, it's easier to understand why and how your website conversion can be improved. The average hotel website has around a 2% conversion rate. Two percent! Imagine 100 people walking into an unstaffed hotel lobby and only two staying.

Why would a guest book direct? Most guests aren't aware of the industry, commissions, etc.—nor do they care.

Guests care about the things that make their experience better; otherwise they might as well book via OTAs. OTAs save time and, because of their brand recognition, are trusted by the consumer.

In order to win direct bookings, you need to offer something the OTAs can't; otherwise there is no reason for the consumer to change their booking habits.

These things can be boiled down into value, service, and staff incentives.

Value
- Make sure your website offers the best rates available—either the same price as OTAs or lower.
- Add incentives like a discount, free upgrades, free breakfast, or special packages available only on the hotel site that will entice the customers to book direct. It doesn't have to cost much for the hotel—you can offer value instead of dropping the rate.
- Educate your guests by recognizing the guest for booking direct. Thank them for booking direct and inform them that this is why they

got a better deal. Show them the price difference — you paid xyz by booking direct, whereas our current public rate is xyz + 10% — or that they will only get access to the best rooms directly through you.

Service, Personalization and Relevancy

Personalization is at the heart of hospitality and I see no reason why you wouldn't offer the same high level of service in your virtual lobby.

- Recognize the returning visitor. Offer welcome back messages or greet them in their own language.
- Display relevant content based on what page they are visiting. For example, if they look at the meeting rooms, send a message after 60 seconds asking if they need help with deciding on a conference room.
- Social proof. As mentioned in the introduction of the book, 95% of people are imitators and only 5% are initiators. People are persuaded more by the actions of others than by any proof we can offer. Display positive reviews and review scores. Tell your website visitors why others buy your products. This will trigger similar buying behaviours within others.
- 20% of travelers have special requests or need help to make complicated reservations. For example, a family may need help to make

sure their rooms are connected or are on the same floor. Make sure you provide them with the tools to contact your hotel; they'll thank you for it and you'll profit.

- Data from Instaroom (www.instaroom.travel) shows that 2-5% of your website visitors want to engage with you through messaging. Add a conversational interface and let smart chatbots greet and engage your website visitors. Data also indicates that up to 40% of all conversations are related to making a complicated booking, which is something your normal booking engine won't be able to handle every time. Don't trust your website visitor to find your email or phone number. You must be there and stay relevant.
- Omnichannel is about being available and looking good on all digital channels. You should have as much attention to detail on your website as at your front desk. Update your website whenever you have new photos, new offers, or special events. When planning on booking a trip, <u>94% of tourists</u> switch between devices, so it's very important that you are mobile friendly and look good everywhere. Display info that guests are looking for and remove the hassle of people calling or emailing. The most frequently asked questions are related to how to get to

the hotel, parking, breakfast, and check-in and check-out. Make sure guests can find these answers easily.
- It's likely that their first visit to your website will be on a smartphone. There are no two ways about it, so you must optimize your website for mobile. Don't make potential guests switch to another device. That's a surefire way to lose them.

The hotel website should be designed to be able to serve all kinds of guests. No matter if they want to book a standard double room, ask about parking facilities before they book, or make a more complicated booking. For example: a family room or a group booking. These are all different guest journeys but they should all feel welcome once they arrive in your virtual lobby. Sit down in your real hotel lobby once in a while just to analyze and observe what kind of guests visit your hotel. Envision the different customer journeys and see how they fit with how your website is designed.

Incentivise Hotel Staff

Make sure you educate and empower your team about what it means to your hotel to get direct bookings.

Employees often don't understand the distribution costs and that OTAs are much more expensive than direct. I can't tell you the number of times I have called a hotel and they quote me a higher price than Booking.com, and when I ask about it, they say they can only give me the quoted price, so I book on Booking.com.

Empower your team to get to the right price with hotel guests and beat external offers—it's better to drop the rate than have the guest book the lower rate elsewhere and pay the commission on top of it.

If guests feel you offer a worse deal, they likely won't book direct again.

Campaigns and Promotions

Promotions and advertising are a great way to find incremental business for your hotel. It is important that you figure out what works for your hotel, while continuing to test new ideas.

When considering setting up a campaign for your hotel, ask yourself the following questions:
Why do I need a promotion or campaign?
When should the campaign be valid? (Travel dates and/or booking dates.)
What should the campaign include? What is your offering? (Room types, other rate inclusions.)

Where should it be available? (Which channels, websites, etc.)
Whom should it be available to? (Will you put any restrictions upon the campaign, such as a minimum length of stay? Should it only be available for specific markets?)

Promotions are a great tool to attract extra demand for slow periods, or just to fly beneath the radar of your competitors. However, remember to plan them well in advance using the five Ws above. Do not set up last-minute promotions with poor fences, which will only cannibalize the same demand that you would have booked anyway.

I believe one of the best types of promotions is one in which you package the room with something else. For example, hotel + flight. The smart thing about this combination is that it allows you to offer a compelling rate, which is only visible to somebody who searches for hotel + flight.

Non-pricing campaigns

Non-pricing refers to the strategy of creating a promotion where you do not offer a discount on your public rates. This is a great tactic to use in order to fly below the radar of your competitors during slow periods.

Here are some examples of how to create a promotion without lowering your public rates:

- Upgrades – offer discounts only on upgraded rooms
- Packages – only offer a discount if the room is booked as part of a package (ex. flight + hotel)
- Double member points
- Added value – offer promotions that include a drink voucher for the hotel bar

Go all in when you create promotions
Do not create a promo and then just sit back and watch what happens. Use all available tools to stimulate as much demand as possible. Depending on which vendors you work with to publish your promos, see if they offer any additional tools that will give your promotions greater visibility. One such example is the Travel Ads tool Expedia offers.

Travel Ads gives you premium placement above the normal list of hotels. You do not pay an extra commission; instead, you pay per click. I have tested this one with a very good return on investment. For example, the last Travel Ad I used returned twenty-five times the amount of money invested in it.

Expedia's Travel Ads also allow you to write your own headline and teaser text, allowing you to get creative and further separate yourself from the competition.

Product Distribution

Product distribution is all about making sure you distribute your products where they should be distributed.

By product, I refer to your hotel rooms and rate types. Here are some great questions to ask yourself:

Did we set up all room types for all channels? Obviously, sometimes it is wise to not distribute all your room types to all channels, but I have learned from experience that when you start this kind of investigation, you end up with a full list of actions and great revenue opportunities.

One example could be that you have some large corporate accounts with only standard rooms attached. What happens when you fill your standard room? Will they search a competitor hotel instead when their booking code says fully booked? Print a Top 50 and make sure you distribute your products wisely to these accounts, partners, and channels.

Do we offer rate parity where we have agreed to do so? Make sure your rate structure is in line with what you have agreed to. A rate monitoring system like OTA Insight can help you stay in control of your rate distribution.

PART 2 - Bonus Chapters

I decided to add in a couple of extra topics which don't necessarily qualify with the "timeless principles" theme of this book. They are, nonetheless, important topics and worth sharing and discussing.

Each bonus chapter is designed as Question and Answer, and these are some of the most common questions I receive on a regular basis regarding revenue management.

Some are borrowed from my first book, *Revenue Superstar!*

Rate Leakage

"How can my hotel be available on all these strange websites with whom I have no direct agreement?"

First, let's look at what rates are actually available online. We can divide them into two different segments: qualified rates and unqualified rates. Qualified means that a potential guest needs to qualify in some way to be able to access the rate. Qualified could mean that in order to get a specific rate they need to also book a flight. The lower room rate is packaged with airfare. Unqualified means the rate is open to anybody. Good examples of unqualified rates are those rates a guest books on Booking.com or through your hotel's own website.

There are also plenty of websites with whom you do not have a direct contract that also offer unqualified rates for your hotel rooms. One example is www.agoda.com, while another is www.hotelsclick.com. These sites often display hotels with old or out-of-date content. From my own experience, customer service is also very poor with these sites.

These minor OTAs can cause severe headaches because they appear in the feeds of metasearch

engines, this can cause additional minor headaches when:
- their rates are lower than those on your own website where you offer a best rate guarantee
- or your hotel's appearance is messy on the hotel-landing page within these search engines. The last thing we want to evoke from our customers is fear or doubt.

Okay, so why is it that OTAs are sometimes able to offer lower rates than the best available rates listed on your own website?

Leakage

There can be two major causes for what I will refer to as leakage.

Static Rates Leakage

Static rates leakage is the more common of the two. This leakage occurs when static net rates are distributed somewhere they should not be.

Allow me to oversimplify to make my point: a possible scenario is that you have a NET/FIT rate agreement with a wholesaler. Let us assume this wholesaler has 1000 partners connected either directly through an interface or manually through a website. One of their partners distributes your room to another player who connects with a minor OTA. Normally you do not want your static rate to be available B2C without qualification because these rates are different from your normal retail rates. In other words, it should not be possible to book that rate unless they qualify for it the correct way. A publicly available website is not a correct way, unless it's packaged with a flight or something similar.

A correct way to sell or distribute a static rate would be, as mentioned, as part of a package, offline (through a travel agent), or within a closed environment. A closed environment could be a membership website for a credit card company with whom guests use your credit card member points to book hotel rooms.

Qualified Dynamic Rates Leakage

Let's say you have a partner to whom you distribute your normal BAR and discounted rates. This could be one of the major OTAs. Here is another oversimplified scenario where this could go wrong:

You set up a promotion on one of your rates that has some restrictions attached to it. This restriction might be that the rate is only available to the South American market. One of the partners within their affiliate network somehow gets hold of the room rate (yes, they have big affiliate networks) and distributes the room to the domestic market in addition to the South American market.

*****

Above are just a few ways leakage can go wrong. This is very difficult to control and unlikely to go away anytime soon. Systems are only becoming increasingly connected; if we want to play within these segments, we must figure out the best structures to avoid as many issues as possible.

It's always very easy to blame somebody else for these issues when they occur, but first of all, we must realize that we are the ones responsible for making sure that we have a good setup in place before we start to find someone else to blame.

Tips and tricks

To finish answering this question, here are some rules and practical tactics for how to think about rate structures and content management.

Rule number one

The world is becoming increasingly connected. If you keep searching for ways to prevent your hotel rooms from being sold on OTAs where you don't have agreements, you will spend a lot of valuable time chasing ghosts. Instead, try to find opportunities within the problem.

Create a good strategy and setup for your rates. For example, if you want to prevent your rates from being sold at a lower rate as a result of leakage, make sure your setup ensures that if this happens it won't affect you that much, and the leakage will be easy for you to identify and take action against.

Again, it all comes down to lead times. Often, you see that these segments where you give static qualified rates normally have different lead times than your normal unqualified rates. If, for example, you see that most of these rates are being sold at least four weeks before arrival, the solution is simple: just set a high rate from the beginning for all the rates in this segment. This then allows you to offer a good early bird discount when rooms in this segment are booked far in advance. By doing this, you avoid having issues zero to thirty days before arrival when most people book online. This is a great way to control your distribution if you need or want to work with qualified static net rates.

Rule number two

Set up good check-in procedures at the hotel. If you have suspicions that a specific wholesaler or website is not obeying the rules that you established for them, be sure to collect reservation confirmation letters during check-in, as but one course of action. Then you can help yourself by helping your partner catch these crooks.

The first ring below represents a possible Qualified Dynamic Rates Leakage, while the next two rings represent possible Static Rates Leakage.

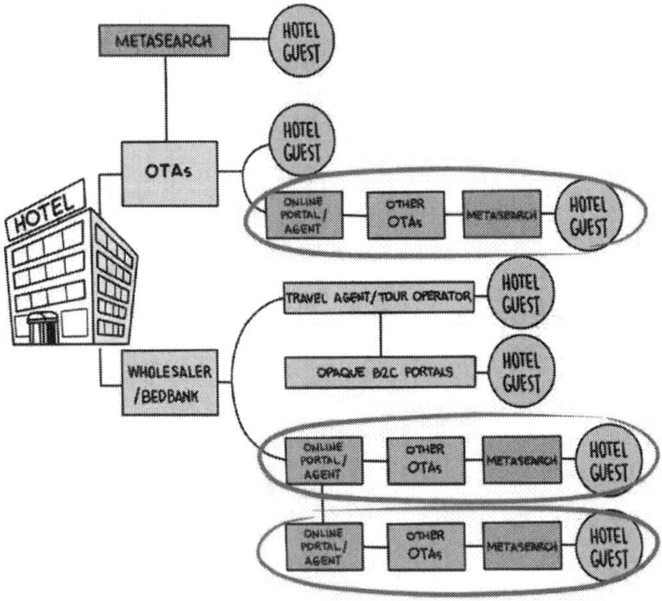
METASEARCH
HOTEL GUEST
HOTEL
OTAs
HOTEL GUEST
ONLINE PORTAL/ AGENT
OTHER OTAs
METASEARCH
HOTEL GUEST
TRAVEL AGENT/TOUR OPERATOR
HOTEL GUEST
OPAQUE B2C PORTALS
HOTEL GUEST
WHOLESALER /BEDBANK
ONLINE PORTAL/ AGENT
OTHER OTAs
METASEARCH
HOTEL GUEST
ONLINE PORTAL/ AGENT
OTHER OTAs
METASEARCH
HOTEL GUEST

What is AI and How Can My Hotel Implement AI?

First, let's define AI (artificial intelligence). The term AI is everywhere right now, and it can be very difficult to see the forest through the trees. What is "true" AI and why is it important for hotels?

You often see that systems offering some kind of automation claim it's AI—although automation alone is good, it's not AI. Automation can, however, be part of an AI process.

Here's my definition of AI:
AI is a process that can automate some processes and improve with time through self-learning (machine learning) and/or human training. The goal is to automate mundane tasks, create new opportunities, or gain actionable insights (and sometimes take advantage of these opportunities without human intervention). AI should be able to learn from data input and give improved data output next time.

That's a broad definition, but it can be boiled down to a simple sentence:
AI is an automatic process that can learn by itself and improve based on user input and other connected databases of historic and future data.

For a more in-depth definition of AI, check out Wikipedia:
https://en.m.wikipedia.org/wiki/Artificial_intelligence

Why is AI such a big deal right now? Simply because it's much more accessible thanks to faster computers, deep learning APIs, and big data (a lot of data available).

Hmm ... so, what can your hotel do about it? The list can grow long, but here are a couple of suggestions.

1. Messaging interface and chatbots
First, some compelling statistics.

One in five of your visitors have special or complicated requests they need answers to.

Up to 88% of the millennial generation prefer messaging to other forms of communication. Text still dominates, even in the age of live video streams.

As mentioned earlier, the average hotel website has around a 2% conversion rate. Two percent! Imagine 100 people walking into an unstaffed hotel lobby and only two staying. This is your website without messaging. By adding messaging, you're upping your level of customer service. Watch conversions grow when customers can interact with you easily.

When planning and booking a trip, 94% of tourists switch between devices.

Outsmart your competitors and offer a seamless way for customers to contact you when they need to. It's likely that their first visit to your website will be on a smartphone.

Data from Instaroom (www.instaroom.travel) shows that around 40% of all conversations are related to new reservations (complicated bookings). The other 50% are related to FAQs.

How is this related to AI?

Once you have embraced messaging and understand that it's here to stay, the next step is to get some help from the world of AI.

Chatbots can be of great assistance. The first thing is to make sure those 50% of FAQs are handheld automatically—not just for the sake of automation but for the sake of improving customer satisfaction and finding new revenue opportunities.

Personalization at scale is suddenly at your fingertip. Imagine a smart agent tapping into the hotel PMS/CRS and other external databases to pull out information to provide the customer with relevant information in real time. I can imagine this chatbot being mentioned in a Tripadvisor review (hehe).

From there the opportunities are endless and can be customized to fit any unique brand, customer journey, or hotel group.

Chatbots will improve with time, and thanks to NLU technology (Natural Language Understanding), the learning curve is steeper than ever.

2. Smart Revenue Management Systems

If you still haven't invested in a smart RM system, it's time to do so. But not necessarily for the reasons you would expect.

I will not go into details about what a smart RM system can do for you, but the principles are the same as previously mentioned. A smart RM system can learn by itself and improve based on user input and connected databases of historic and future data. In other words, the output will improve with time. The result? Ever better pricing recommendations.

Now there are a bunch of pricing, yield, and rate intelligence systems using AI. You should check these out as well. Just let me know if you need some direction.

So, what is the unexpected reason to invest in a smart RM system?

Obviously, the smart RM system will help you increase revenues by optimizing pricing and recommendations. I do, however, think it opens an even greater opportunity, and that is for the revenue manager to be able to focus on the big revenue-related tasks like action-based forecasting, deep analysis, online content improvement, and customer journey analysis (this is not yet as easily replaced by AI).

How Can I Increase My Average Rates?

"For every action, there is an equal and opposite reaction."
Isaac Newton

You have to love this question. How can you increase your ADR? This question can be answered with one simple rule, which goes like this: the only way to increase ADR is by doing things that do not lower it. This is probably not the answer you expected, but the best way to solve this problem is to inverse how you look at it.

Here is a good way to *not* lower your ADR.

The 20% Rule

What 20% of your business stands for 80% of your revenue? Figure out what segment, channels, rate category, or companies qualify for this and double down on your optimization directed specifically toward it.

Set action to what effects a big chunk of your business instead of directing your attention to everything. This will create momentum to increase your ADR.

Here are some thoughts on what to consider once you know what business to focus on.

Price and Rate Strategies

The paradox here is normally that if you increase rates, you will receive less demand from these channels. If you receive less demand from your best ADR channels, your ADR will decrease. Find ways to stimulate incremental business instead. To do this, consider the following:

Automation

Create automated rate restriction strategies. Set up a system that helps you set the best pricing restrictions. This will free up time so you can focus on the 20% Rule. Review your automatic pricing set-ups once a month and change them when and where it is necessary.

Price Points

How strong is the correlation between higher BAR rates and declining demand for your hotel? Make sure you are not missing crucial price points in your rate setup. See BAR section on page 30 for more details.

Reference Price and Prospect Theory

What we do not want is to create a reference price that is lower than it should be. The reference price is what the customer expects the price to be based on memories of past prices, prices set by brand leaders, related products, or the way a price is presented.

If you discount a room too much, you might risk lowering your hotel reference price. Be careful how you restrict prices through such things as promotions. A simple way to increase your reference price could be to display your rooms differently. Start with the upgraded room type(s), followed by your standard room type(s). When displayed in reverse like this, a potential guest might see this as a savings instead of a loss. You should definitely conduct some experiments here to figure out what would work best in your particular circumstances.

Daniel Kahneman won a Nobel Prize in Economics for his work developing Prospect Theory. Prospect Theory states that people make decisions based on the potential value of losses and gains rather than the final outcome. In other words, loss hurts an individual more than the equivalent gain makes him or her feel good. Once you understand the behavioral aspects of human decision-making, the possibilities are endless.

The takeaway, if nothing else, is to never stop experimenting to figure out what works and what doesn't work.

Promotions: The 100 Rule

Make your current offers more appealing to potential guests by applying The 100 Rule. This rule states that when a product's price is greater than 100 (regardless of currency), use absolute value to market a discount. When the opposite is true (the price is less than 100) use a percentage to market a discount.

> Imagine a hotel room sells for $500 a night
> A three-night stay = $1500
> Promotional Discount: 10% off a three-night stay
> Absolute value = Save $150
> Percentage value = Save 10%
> Which one sounds more appealing to you, the absolute value discount or the percentage value discount? (Remember, the discount amount is the same.)
>
> Now imagine a bottle of wine sells for $40
> Promotional Discount: 10% off
> Absolute value = Save $4
> Percentage value = Save 10%
> Which one sounds more appealing to you now, the absolute value discount or the percentage discount?

The above examples of The 100 Rule demonstrate that how people perceive an offer depends on how it is framed. Something as simple as framing a promotion's value in absolute terms rather than as a percentage, or vice versa, brings psychology to bear on how people determine whether or not to make a purchase. Consider this rule the next time you set up a campaign or plan a promotion. If you want to read more about The 100 Rule and other cool concepts, I highly recommend the book *Contagious, How To Build Word Of Mouth In The Digital Age* by Jonah Berger.

*****

Obviously, there are many more ways to increase your ADR than just the examples I provided in this chapter, but I hope this gives you some additional inspiration and tools to begin tackling your specific ADR challenge.

WHICH ONE WOULD YOU CHOOSE?

Save 10% | Save $150

Stay 3 nights save 10%
BOOK

Stay 3 nights save $150
BOOK

What Are Some Good Tricks to Increase My Room Sales Profit Margin?

"Sometimes the questions are complicated and the answers are simple."
Dr. Seuss

This one is actually very easy. Print out a top-50 list of who or what contributes most to your room sales. Start from the top of the list and set up actions for how to increase profit margins for each channel, account, and rate. The only difficulty here is in overcoming your own potential procrastination that prevents you from actually taking action on your action points!

Imagine if your hotel has a partner that contributes to 10% of all your room sales. What happens if you come up with something that could increase your margin by 1%? How much revenue is that? This is a no-brainer, but what can you actually change?

Suggested actions for improving room sales profit

Compensation negotiation
Come up with a good simulation that demonstrates how both parties (your hotel and your partners) can profit from lowering commissions by a certain

percentage. A potential way to frame this would be to offer a partner more room availability in return for decreasing their commission.

More room types = more availability and choice

Make sure your biggest accounts have access to as many of your room types as possible on the hotel's landing page. This will generate higher ADRs for this account and thus higher profit.

More for less

Find channels with the best profit margin for your hotel; see if you can compromise your rate to stimulate more sales. If you do this right and proactively replace this rate with lower margin rates, it will help you to increase your overall profit margin.

Content and relevancy

There is an entire chapter devoted to just this topic because it is so extremely important.

What Are the Best Ways to Deliver Professional Reports When Lacking Computer Skills?

Acknowledging what you don't know is the dawning of wisdom.
Charlie Munger

This is more normal than you think, but luckily, there is help available.

You can learn a great deal simply by taking online courses and watching YouTube videos. It doesn't matter if it's for Excel, PowerPoint, or something else entirely. Invest some time in yourself. In addition to learning new computer skills, an added bonus is that taking this initiative will make you look good in front of your boss.

Remember, there are also websites where you can buy entire compilations of PowerPoint templates. As Pablo Picasso said: *"Good artists copy, great artists steal."*

Beyond learning computer skills related to specific software, there are also free revenue management courses available that you should look into.

Ways to invest in yourself

Below is a list of sources you can use to strengthen your computer and professional skills.

Class Central
This is a search engine for online courses (paid and free). You can browse subjects, search topics, or see trending courses.
www.class-central.com

Udemy
Twenty-four million students use Udemy, and they offer 80,000+ courses. This website is my personal favorite.
www.udemy.com

Coursera
Free online courses from top universities around the world. Their tagline is: "Build in-demand skills and earn valuable credentials."
www.coursera.com

edX
Take free online courses from the best universities and institutions in the world—Harvard, MIT, UC Berkeley, Microsoft, Tsinghua University, The Smithsonian, and more.
www.edx.org

Lynda
Paid membership gives you access to everything. Lynda is owned by LinkedIn.
www.lynda.com

YouTube
We all know YouTube. Most things you want to learn can be found here — free of charge.
www.youtube.com

Envato Market
Download cool PowerPoint templates here. This site offers ready-to-use design assets from more than 14,000 independent creators.
https://graphicriver.net/presentation-templates/powerpoint-templates

Recommended Reads for Revenue Managers

I have discovered that it is wise to also study other fields which don't necessarily have a direct relationship with revenue management but which can still inspire you and connect dots and ideas which you would never considered otherwise. Here is a short list with some of my highest recommendations. Adopting multiple mental models from other fields will give you a competitive edge and see things others might miss.

In a famous speech in the 1990s, Charlie Munger (American investor, businessman, & philanthropist) summed up the approach to practical wisdom through understanding mental models by saying: "Well, the first rule is that you can't really know anything if you just remember isolated facts and try and bang 'em back. If the facts don't hang together on a latticework of theory, you don't have them in a usable form. You've got to have models in your head. And you've got to array your experience both vicarious and direct on this latticework of models. You may have noticed students who just try to remember and pound back what is remembered. Well, they fail in school and in life. You've got to hang experience on a latticework of models in your head."

Misbehaving: The Making of Behavioral Economics by Richard Thaler
Richard Thaler has spent his career studying the notion that humans are central to the economy — and that we're error-prone individuals, not Spock-like automatons. Now behavioural economics is hugely influential, changing the way we think not just about money, but about ourselves, our world, and all kinds of everyday decisions. Whether buying an alarm clock, selling football tickets, or applying for a mortgage, we all succumb to biases and make decisions that deviate from the standards of rationality assumed by economists. In other words, we misbehave.

Deep Work: Rules for Focused Success in a Distracted World by Cal Newport
Many modern knowledge workers now spend most of their brain power battling distraction and interruption, whether because of the incessant pinging of devices, noisy open-plan offices, or the difficulty of deciding what deserves your attention the most. When Cal Newport coined the term "deep work" on his popular blog, Study Hacks, in 2012, he found the concept quickly hit a nerve. Most of us, after all, are excruciatingly familiar with shallow

work instead — distractedly skimming the surface of our workload and never getting to the important part.

Contagious: Why Things Catch on by Jonah Berger
The New York Times bestseller that explains why certain products and ideas become popular. "Jonah Berger knows more about what makes information 'go viral' than anyone in the world" (Daniel Gilbert, author of the bestseller *Stumbling on Happiness*). What makes things popular? If you said advertising, think again. People don't listen to advertisements, they listen to their peers. But why do people talk about certain products and ideas more than others? Why are some stories and rumors more infectious? And what makes online content go viral?

Influence: The Psychology of Persuasion by Robert B. Cialdini
Influence, the classic book on persuasion, explains the psychology of why people say "yes" — and how to apply these understandings. Dr. Robert Cialdini is the seminal expert in the rapidly expanding field of influence and persuasion. His thirty-five years of rigorous, evidence-based research along with a three-year program of study on what moves people to change behavior has resulted in this highly acclaimed book.

You'll learn the six universal principles, how to use them to become a skilled persuader, and how to defend yourself against them. Perfect for people in all walks of life, the principles of Influence will move you toward profound personal change and act as a driving force for your success.

Superforecasting: The Art and Science of Prediction by Philip E. Tetlock and Dan Gardner
Everyone would benefit from seeing further into the future, whether buying stocks, crafting policy, launching a new product, or simply planning the week's meals. Unfortunately, people tend to be terrible forecasters. As Wharton professor Philip Tetlock showed in a landmark 2005 study, even experts' predictions are only slightly better than chance. However, an important and underreported conclusion of that study was that some experts do have real foresight, and Tetlock has spent the past decade trying to figure out why. What makes some people so good? And can this talent be taught?

Glossary of Terms

Average Daily Rate (ADR) – A measure of the average room rate paid per rooms sold. To calculate ADR, divide room revenue by rooms sold.

Average Length of Stay (ALOS) – A measure of the total room nights in a hotel (or in a specific segment) per the number of total reservations in the hotel. To calculate ALOS, divide total occupied room nights by total bookings.

Average Rate Index (ARI) – A measure to determine whether the hotel realizes its fair share of ADR compared to a competitive set. To calculate ARI, divide the hotel's ADR by the ADR of a competitive set (that is representative of the market). An ARI equal to 1.00 indicates that the hotel has secured an equal share of revenue based on ADR compared to the competitive set. An ARI above 1.00 indicates a hotel has secured a greater share. An ARI below 1.00 indicates that the hotel has secured a lesser share. Multiply ARI by 100 or convert it to a percentage to ease the burden of working with this measurement.

Best Available Rate (BAR) – The lowest unqualified rate for a room type available to the general public. BAR provides a guarantee that guests will not find a lower rate for the same room type on a given night(s) on an OTA or elsewhere. This is also a common rate used for rate comparisons between hotels.

Booking curve – A tool that can visually represent bookings over time, incorporating data such as pickup, number of bookings, availability and yielding capacity of the hotel.

Booking window or Booking lead-time – The time period between when a hotel reservation is made and a guest's actual arrival date. Measures how far in advance rooms are booked.

Block / Group pricing – A non-yieldable rate applied to a fixed number of rooms reserved for a specified group. A window exists during which members of the specified group must book their rooms in order to receive the non-yieldable rate.

Break-even – The point at which revenues equal costs.

Budget – Establishes a hotel's financial plan for the upcoming calendar or fiscal year. Generally, it should designate a daily occupancy, ADR and RevPAR for every major market segment. It outlines percentage changes over previous years, both by month and by quarter. This annual budget comprises part of the overall financial budget for the hotel.

Capacity – The number of rooms a hotel has to offer.

Central Reservation System (CRS) – A system to manage the booking process and existing reservations, and to maintain hotel information and data, including rates and inventory. Systems can either be created in-house or by a third-party vendor.

Channel management – The techniques and systems hotels use to update hotel information, room inventory and rates in each of their distribution channels.

Channels – The different means by which potential guests can reserve or book a hotel room.

Closed to arrival (CTA) – An inventory control mechanism used by revenue managers to prevent new reservations being made by guest arriving on a specific date. The only guests permitted to use such inventory are those arriving at earlier dates and remaining over the CTA date.

Cold/slow periods – A period of time (season, month, day, or time of day) when operating performance (demand) is low. Cold periods are times when revenue managers might discount rates or offer incentives in an attempt to increase occupancy and improve RevPAR.

Commission – The payment that a travel agent or other third party receives for each reservation made through their office or site.

Competitive set (or Compset) – Consists of a group of hotels recognized as direct competitors to the hotel by which the hotel can compare itself against the group's aggregate performance.

Conversion – The process of a guest moving from gathering information about a hotel or shopping for a room to taking action by making direct inquiries or finalizing a booking.

Conversion Rate (CR) – A statistical measure of the number of people who click an ad who eventually make a purchase associated with that ad. To calculate CR, divide the total number of buyers by the total number of unique clicks.

Cost Per Click (CPC) – The average cost to an advertiser incurred as a result of a consumer clicking an online ad.

Click Through Rate (CTR) – A measure of the total number of webpage impressions that result in clicks, representing the number of people who actually see an advertisement. To calculate CTR, divide the total number of clicks by the total number of unique impressions.

Demand – The amount of interest in a hotel, including in its beds, rooms, event spaces, etc.

Denial – A response to a potential guest's request stating that a hotel cannot accommodate any additional guests because it is fully booked or a restriction has been placed on the date requested.

Displacement Analysis – An analysis conducted to determine whether it's prudent to take rooms out of a hotel's inventory—usually to accommodate a group's request—that could be requested later at a higher rate by late-booking or walk-in guests. To conduct a displacement analysis, multiply the number of rooms denied by the average rate for that segment of business. If the resulting number is higher than the group revenue, then the group's request should be denied.

Dynamic pricing – A method hotels employ to help optimize profitability by changing prices for a room or service in response to changes in capacity, competition, demand and other guest attributes.

Elastic demand – When consumer demand responds to price changes. Factors that can influence elastic demand include increased competition, standardized services and perceived luxury.

Fenced rate – A rate that offers benefits to potential guests, but with conditions or requirements that apply in order to secure a reservation. To procure such a rate, reservations are often nonrefundable, purchased in advance and cannot be canceled.

Fixed pricing – A pricing strategy in which prices do not fluctuate based on demand, product characteristics or segmentation within markets.

Forecast – A prediction of the number of rooms that can be sold on a specific date or period of time. Accurate forecasting greatly enhances other revenue management strategies according to the expected level of demand.

Generic search – A search for a product in which the user does not enter a brand name as a keyword. When searching for a hotel, a user might type "downtown hotels in Boston," when seeking information about hotels in the Boston area, rather than specify a known hotel or chain.

Global Distribution Systems (GDS) – Four of the most recognized reservation systems in the industry: Amadeus, Galileo, Sabre and Worldspan.

Gross Operating Profit Per Available Room (GOPPAR) – A measure of total revenue less operational and marketing expenses per room used to measure a hotel's performance and to make adjustments accordingly. To calculate GOPPAR, subtract operational/marketing expenses per room from the total revenue brought in by rooms sold.

Group Displacement – A process of measuring a group's total profitability compared to the profitability of gaining business from other channels that would otherwise be displaced by the group.

Group forecasting – Making educated estimates for how many group block rooms will be booked and when, based on previous booking data.

Group Pricing – *See Block / Group Pricing*

Group segment mix – The proportions of the different group segments that comprise the total group business for the hotel. In general, these segments receive different rates.

Inelastic demand – When consumer demand does not respond to prices changes. Factors that can influence inelastic demand are reduced competition, differentiated services and consumer staples.

Landing page – The "front page" of a site a web user first arrives at as a result of clicking on a listing's link in a search.

Last room availability clause (LRA) – A contract clause—often agreed upon between the hotel and third-party agents—indicating that the contracted rate is available as long as rooms of any type remain available.

Leisure traveler – A traveler who travels for personal

reasons rather than for work. Leisure travelers are not business travelers.

Length of stay – The number of nights a guest has booked at the hotel.

Length-of-stay controls – Controls put in place to help regulate demand for rooms in an effort to organize and optimize occupancy for a hotel.

Market Penetration Index (MPI) – A measure to help the hotel recognize its position in proportion to its competition by determining whether the hotel realizes its fair share of occupancy. To calculate MPI, divide the occupancy percentage of the hotel by the occupancy percentage of the competitive set (that is representative of the market). An MPI equal to 1.00 indicates that the hotel has secured an equal share of occupancy compared to the competitive set. An MPI above 1.00 indicates a hotel has secured a greater share of occupancy. An MPI below 1.00 indicates that the hotel has secured a lesser share of occupancy. Multiply MPI by 100 or convert it to a percentage to ease the burden of working with this measurement.

Metasearch engine – A website that can search all OTAs on behalf of a consumer and display the best available prices based on predefined criteria.

Net rate – The sell rate with commissions sometimes required by third-parties (namely, OTAs) already subtracted.

Occupancy – A measure of the percentage of available rooms sold during a specific period of time. To calculate occupancy, divide the number of rooms sold by rooms available.

Occupancy Index – A measure of the hotel's occupancy percentage compared to the occupancy percentage of the competitive set (that is representative of the market). To calculate the occupancy index, divide the hotel occupancy percentage by the occupancy percentage of the competitive set, then multiply by 100.

Online Travel Agency (OTA) – A web-based hotel and travel reservations system. Hotels offer inventory to OTAs, which sell rooms in exchange for a commission.

Opaque – Describes a booking channel that shields the identity of a hotel until a guest completes their reservation. It can also describe channels where guests must first become members to gain access to special rates.

Overbooking – A tactic of booking reservations beyond capacity to offset cancelled reservations and no-shows.

Pace – *See Pickup*

Pay Per Click (PPC) – An Internet advertising model where advertisers use ad links to direct traffic from host websites to their own websites or products. Advertisers pay the owners of host websites a fee each time an ad of theirs is clicked.

Perishable inventory – Inventory, that if not used within a specific period of time, becomes a lost revenue opportunity. A hotel room is perishable inventory.

Pickup / Pace – The rate at which reservations are booked for a specific date.

Price Elasticity – A measure showing how demand for a room responds to a change in its price.

Property Management System (PMS) – A hotel's onsite system that facilitates management processes for the hotel, including guest check-in and check-out.

Rate parity – A guarantee that potential guests will be quoted the same price for the same product regardless of where they shop. It allows individual hotels and chains to set the same price for each of their room types across all distribution channels.

Reference price – The price consumers think a service, product or room should cost. Points of reference for prices include the price last paid, the price most frequently paid, the price other consumers have paid for the same thing, or market prices and posted prices.

Regression – A statistical analysis for evaluating the relationships that exist among variables. It measures the association between one variable (the dependent variable) and one or more other variables (the independent variables), usually formulated in an equation.

Reputation management – Influencing and controlling an individual's or business's reputation, particularly as it appears online or through social media.

Revenue Generating Index (RGI) – *See RevPAR Index (RPI)*

Revenue Management – The art and science of predicting real-time customer demand and optimizing the price and availability of products to match that demand.

RevPAR Index (RPI) – A measure to determine whether the hotel realizes its fair share of revenue compared to a competitive set. To calculate RPI, divide the RevPAR of the hotel by the RevPAR of the competitive set (that is representative of the market). An RPI equal to 1.00 indicates that the hotel has secured its fair share of revenue compared to hotels it the competitive set. An RPI above 1.00 indicates the hotel has secured a greater share. An RPI below 1.00 indicates that the hotel has secured a lesser share. Multiply RPI by 100 or convert it to a percentage to ease the burden of working with this measurement.

RevPATI – Revenue per available time-based inventory unit. RevPAR and RevPASH are variations on this measure. RevPATI is calculated differently depending on the context. It is used in all applications of revenue management to analyze a hotel's or chain's ability to optimize its revenue capacity.

Revenue per available room (RevPAR) – A measure of how well a hotel manages its inventory and rates in order to optimize revenue. To calculate, multiply occupancy by ADR.

Search engine optimization (SEO) – The process of maximizing unique visitors to a website by improving the site's position in organic search results.

Segmented markets – Markets composed of consumers bearing similar characteristics. Segments can be comprised based on consumers' ages, purchasing power, frequency of purchase, and affiliation to groups; or be differentiated by how much they are willing to pay for a service, product or room.

Shoulder Date – Dates that fall directly beside or very close to other high demand dates. A Friday and a Sunday are each considered shoulder dates when they are not sold out, but the Saturday between them is.

Stay Pattern Management – The process of optimizing hotel capacity by ensuring the stay patterns on the books do not result in unsellable stay patterns remaining to be booked.

Time-variable demand – Uncertain demand that varies by time of year, day of week, in relation to holidays, etc.

Transient – Non-group or non-committed business (guests). These guests are largely on-the-move and seeking short stays.

Unconstrained Demand – A forecast of the quantity of rooms a hotel could sell if had an unlimited number of rooms—that is, no constraints or limits.

Variable pricing – Simultaneously offering varying prices at different points-of-sale (including websites) for the same service, product or room.

Wash – The fraction of the group block that the group does not materialize.

Win rates – The rate at which potential guests accept offers.

Worldspan – GDS system originally designed for airlines, now widely used by travel agents to book all forms of travel.

Yield – Revenue made. Includes the dynamic pricing, overbooking and allocation of perishable assets necessary to maximize revenue.

Yield Management – Synonymous with Revenue Management, the purpose of Yield Management is to maximize revenue and profits. The process involves understanding, anticipating and reacting to guests' needs and behavior, with the intention of increasing yield.

Works Cited

"Advertise with Search, Display and More - Microsoft Advertising." Bing Ads. Accessed December 04, 2018. https://advertising.microsoft.com/en/WWDocs/User/display/cl/ researchreport/ 31966/en/.

"Artificial Intelligence." Wikipedia. December 04, 2018. Accessed December 04, 2018. https://en.m.wikipedia.org/wiki/Artificial_intelligence.

Investopedia. "Average Daily Rate - ADR." Investopedia. January 17, 2018. Accessed December 04, 2018. https://www.investopedia.com/terms/a/average-daily-rate.asp.

Berger, Jonah. *Contagious: How to Build Word of Mouth in the Digital Age.* London: Simon & Schuster, 2014.

Berger, Jonah. *Contagious: Why Things Catch On.* New York ; London ; Toronto ; Sydney ; New Delhi: Simon & Schuster Paperbacks, 2016.

"Big Data, for Better or Worse: 90% of World's Data Generated over Last Two Years." ScienceDaily. May 22, 2013. Accessed December 04, 2018. https://www.sciencedaily.com/releases/2013/05/130522085217.htm.

Cialdini, Robert B. *Influence: The Psychology of Persuasion*. New York: Collins, 2007.

"Cornell Study Demonstrates ROI of Social Media and Reviews." TripAdvisor. August 14, 2018. Accessed December 04, 2018. https://www.tripadvisor.com/TripAdvisorInsights/ n724/cornell-study-demonstrates-roi-social-media-and-reviews.

Investopedia. "Economist." Investopedia. July 25, 2018. Accessed December 04, 2018. http://www.investopedia.com/terms/e/economist.asp.

"Finding The Balance Between "OTAs" (Online Travel Agents) & Direct Bookings." Pebble Design - Trusted Leaders in Hotel Web Design. Accessed December 04, 2018. https://pebbledesign.com/insights/finding-the-balance-between-otas-and-direct-bookings.

Hammer, Johan. *Revenue Superstar!: The Simple Rules of Hotel Revenue Management*. S.l.: Johan Hammer, 2016.

"Instaroom | Connecting Hotels with Travelers." Instaroom | Connecting Hotels with Travelers. Accessed December 04, 2018. http://www.instaroom.travel/.

Lewis, C. S., and Pauline Baynes. *The Chronicles of Narnia*. New York: Macmillan, 1988.

Newport, Cal. *Deep Work: Rules for Focused Success in a Distracted World*. S.l.: Grand Central Pub, 2018.

Investopedia. "Revenue Per Available Room - RevPAR." Investopedia. October 21, 2018. Accessed December 04, 2018. www.investopedia.com/terms/r/revpar.asp.

Tetlock, Philip, and Dan Gardner. *Superforecasting: The Art and Science of Prediction*. London: Random House Books, 2016.

Thaler, Richard. *Misbehaving: The Making of Behavioral Economics*. Plaats Van Uitgave Niet Vastgesteld: Penguin Books, 2016.

Thiel, Peter. *Zero to One: Notes on Startups, or How to Build the Future*. London: Virgin Books, 2014.

"Travel Booking Trends Revealed in Let's-Book-It Moments." Google. Accessed December 04, 2018. https://www.thinkwithgoogle.com/marketing-resources/micro-moments/travel-booking-trends-book-it-moments/.

"Upgrade the Guest Experience." ReviewPro. Accessed December 04, 2018. http://www.reviewpro.com/.

Viewpoints. "In Defence of Online Travel Agencies - They Are Not Evil." Tnooz. March 31, 2014. Accessed December 04, 2018. https://www.tnooz.com/article/online-travel-agencies-not-evil-iceportal/.

Note pages

Now it's your turn to create some timeless principles. Take the time to write down your own findings and strategies as you go through your own carrier. This is a good way to make this book even more personal and complete.

Johan Hammer

Johan Hammer

Revenue Management

Johan Hammer

Revenue Management

Printed in Great Britain
by Amazon